Renee & By

# THROUGH THE EYE
# OF THE EAGLE

May you discover the
Magick between each
Page
It was wonderful meeting
such fairy folk.
Red Kelly

# THROUGH THE EYE OF THE EAGLE

## The Legend of Eau Claire Gorge

Rod Kelly

Note for Librarians: a cataloguing record for this book that includes Dewey Decimal Classification and US Library of Congress numbers is available from the Library and Archives of Canada. The complete cataloguing record can be obtained from their online database at:
www.collectionscanada.ca/amicus/index-e.html
ISBN 1-4120-5783-3
Printed in Victoria, BC, Canada

A special thanks to Debbie Briatico for her masterful job of editing this book.

*Printed on paper with minimum 30% recycled fibre. Trafford's print shop runs on "green energy" from solar, wind and other environmentally-friendly power sources.*

# TRAFFORD

*Offices in Canada, USA, Ireland and UK*
This book was published *on-demand* in cooperation with Trafford Publishing. On-demand publishing is a unique process and service of making a book available for retail sale to the public taking advantage of on-demand manufacturing and Internet marketing. On-demand publishing includes promotions, retail sales, manufacturing, order fulfilment, accounting and collecting royalties on behalf of the author.

**Book sales for North America and international:**
Trafford Publishing, 6E–2333 Government St.,
Victoria, BC v8t 4p4  CANADA
phone 250 383 6864 (toll-free 1 888 232 4444)
fax 250 383 6804; email to orders@trafford.com
**Book sales in Europe:**
Trafford Publishing (uk) Ltd., Enterprise House, Wistaston Road Business Centre,
Wistaston Road, Crewe, Cheshire cw2 7rp  UNITED KINGDOM
phone 01270 251 396 (local rate 0845 230 9601)
facsimile 01270 254 983; orders.uk@trafford.com
**Order online at:**
trafford.com/05-0683
10  9  8  7  6  5  4  3  2

## DEDICATION

I'd like to dedicate this book to three special people who enabled me to write about this interesting topic, while helping me fulfill my spiritual journey—my loving wife, Ann, for her devoted encouragement; Laurie Anderson, who introduced me to this glorious land, and particularly Eau Claire Gorge; and Barrett Maxwell for his unselfish honesty, which helped validate my decision to move into the home of Wishna-hea and all the wondrous spirits of this book.

# Chapter 1

*"I soared high above the treetops and with a single beat of my wings I flew upward and into the lofty clouds. Like a blanket, the clouds blocked the brilliant Grandfather Sun from the Earth. Soon I passed through the darkness and after many beats of my wings, I began my flight into the warmth and purity of the Grandfather's light. My journey was long, but I finally entered the home of Manitou to deliver my report and receive my instructions for the day."*

*"Through His wisdom He sanctioned me to become His eyes over the spirits of both man and beast in the wilderness below. My eyesight is superior to any of the creatures of either Father Sky or Mother Earth's domain. My wingspan is great, and allows me to pass easily beyond the earthly world. The Great One has allowed me to master both instinct and insight, so that I may better serve Him."*

The long winter had finally conceded to the warmth of spring. This was the first victory day for the winds of change. Soon the sun would lose its nearly unobstructed view of the Earth beneath the oak and maple forest. The hardwoods shared the forest with massive white pines that towered high above the bush.

A chorus of the forest's birds was beginning to sing its morning song to Grandfather Sun, and announce their return to the inhabitants of the bush. They were delighted to once again share their springtime home. The branches of the trees were once again breathing life and yielding to the ways of nature.

The songbirds' welcome echoed as the light of the mid-April sun filtered through the forest and awakened all of the creatures—from the great bears to the smallest chipmunks. Even the North wind had lost its ferocity and became a gentle breeze. Only small patches of snow remained on the northern slopes. The winter had been warm and the snows were light.

As the bright morning light graced the new day, Wishna-hea smiled as she looked to the East to welcome the sun. Even though it had been a mild winter, she was anxious to feel the warmth of the spring season. She was excited that it had finally arrived. With a few well-placed twigs and branches, she lit the fire pit, which soon danced to life with flames. Before she started to prepare her man's morning meal, she once again faced the East and began her ritualistic prayer to Mother Earth.

She took out a pinch of tobacco from the pouch that hung around her neck and sprinkled it upon the fire. As she knelt down, Wishna-hea raised her hands above her head and focused her eyes on a passing cloud. She opened her mind, body and spirit to the forces of nature. As she faced the East she prayed: "I give thanks to the East, for it is the home of Grandfather Sun, who gave life to our world. It is also the home of my Spirit Brother, the Elk, who has chosen to be my protectorate spirit and teacher."

She then turned to the South and continued: "I give thanks to the South for it is the home of the Summer Sun, who gives bounty to all the lands of our home. It is also the home of our Red Brothers, the caretakers of our world. My Turtle Spirit, who has chosen to be my teacher in the ways of Mother Earth, also dwells there."

Her prayer was long, but it was the same prayer that protected her mother and previous generations, as they survived and thrived in a land that had tested their faith, stamina and strength. In fact, the prayer was as old as the history of her people. She continued: "I give thanks to the West, for it is the home of our ancestors, who share the teachings of the Ancient Ones with us, for they are the caretakers and they teach us introspection. It is the home of our Black Brothers, as well as my Bear Spirit, who has chosen to be my protector and companion all the days of my life."

She now turned to the direction of the North and said: "I give thanks to the North, the home of the Great Bear of Winter, who has spared our people this season by allowing his fury to remain at bay. It is the home of our White Brothers, and of Wisdom, as well as my Snake Spirit, who allows me to understand change and the medicines of our lands, and protects me from all enemies. I humbly give thanks to the Upper World, the Middle World, and the Underworld, for they are my connection to the past, present and future."

When she finished her morning prayers, she tossed a small handful of tobacco into the coals of the sacred fire. She spoke softly and then closed her eyes, bowing her head. As she closed her mind to all earthly things, she envisioned her words as they floated high above the clouds towards the land of her ancestors. She watched as her words drifted through the waterfall that marked the entrance of His home. Knowing that her prayers had arrived safely, she filled with a warm sense of well-being.

Since becoming Weenuk's woman, she had been allowed to witness the magnificent waters of Manitou's home and feel its powers. As spiritual leader of their people, Weenuk was the only one who was permitted to pass through the land of Manitou. Some day, she, too, would be permitted to enter, but for now, she only watched from a distance. She released her vision and returned back to her conscious thoughts.

She whistled to the birds high in the treetops, and her sounds echoed as sweetly as theirs. She closed her eyes and felt an infusion of joy. The long winter was gone and the warm breezes of the growing season would soon be here.

She had passed fifteen winters and was always grateful to welcome easier days. It was believed that when the sun looked at the Earth longer, the Earth's belly was warmed—the warmer the belly, the better the disposition. This explained the seasons of the great North.

The village of the Montagnais comprised of many lodges, and like the spokes of a great wheel, they spread out around the lodge of Weenuk, the Sachem. Next to his lodge was the lodge of the Chief, who was highly honored and respected by all the people, for he was wise and his punishments were just.

The Chief, Amable du Fond, often called on Weenuk to tell him about the wisdom of their ancestors, because it was believed that Weenuk was the only one who could converse directly with Manitou, who reigned over all the lands and skies of the Algonquin tribes. The lands of the Montagnais comprised of many villages, but this was the largest.

Traditionally, the Montagnais had been primarily hunter-gatherers, but for the past few generations, they had learned to plant crops from their neighbors, the Nipissing's. Some of the women had been chosen to tend to small crops of corn, beans and squash, as a means of supplementing the diminishing elk and moose population. Their farming enabled them to survive even the harshest winters. A separate field was set aside for the sacred herbs of tobacco, sage and sweet grass. As they farmed the land, they strengthened their connection with the spirits, especially Manitou.

The forests provided much bounty with massive Cedar trees that would take two grown men to wrap their arms around. The River of Clear Waters had been renamed to honor the powerful Chief, and meandered through the village, providing food and transportation for everyone. Since the French introduction into the area, the guardian of the Spirit of the River had been renamed Eau Claire Gorge. This majestic gorge and the lands around it gave the Montagnais great power.

Since she was a child, Wishna-hea enjoyed waking up before everyone else and going into the forest to wait for the sunrise. Even in the middle of the harsh North winters when the trees would pop from the severe cold, she would bundle herself up in the furs of red deer or moose, and trudge through the newly fallen snow. She would make her way to the river and pay homage to the Spirit of Clear Waters.

"The others will be rising soon," she thought to herself. Her pace quickened as she placed the last log on the fire, which now burned warmly. She turned to the river and scampered to the water's edge. She pulled her dress over her head and dropped it onto the ground. With three short steps, she dove in and glided effortlessly through the water. As the water's cool temperature shocked her naked flesh, she kicked her legs in an effort to propel herself more quickly. The ice had only melted less than two weeks ago.

During her swim, she allowed her spirit to blend with the water. It had been a long time since she visited the river. Her body quickly adjusted to the cold and permitted her spirit to relish the moment. She dove deep beneath the water's surface again and again. She wished the fish were not so frightened, because she loved swimming among them. Only after she held her breath for a long time did their inquisitive nature allow them to come out and see what caused so much commotion.

She often practiced holding her breath throughout the winter, so she could remain with the fishes and frogs longer. She preferred swimming beneath the surface because it also helped her to avoid the watchful eyes of anyone wandering by the river. She had become aware of a bunch of young men, and even old men, who enjoyed watching her swimming naked. The blanket of water concealed her most of the time and that pleased her spirit.

Her body turned and twisted in a ritualistic dance. She gracefully moved through the water. The sensation of the cold water stimulated her entire existence. The river was truly her source of strength and wisdom.

She drew the new air in slowly and filled her lungs to capacity. Motionless, she remained afloat. Slowly her breath was released and another was taken. Like a beautiful wood sculpture her body floated as peacefully as a leaf.

From high above, the Eagle circled and observed her closely. Manitou had commanded the Eagle to watch over and protect her. The Hawk and the Owl also assisted the Eagle by increasing its ability to watch over Wishna-hea at night and in dense forests.

Her thoughts glided back to her seventh summer when she had been given the name of Sheeta, which meant Little One. As she grew a little older, she began to resent the restrictive name. It was not until years later when Weenuk was asked to give her a new name—one that properly suited her. During the special naming ceremony, the entire tribe bustled with excitement. There was much speculation about what she would be called. She was a child who always warmed everyone's hearts with smiles and laughter.

Her energy was boundless as she danced and sang around the tribal fire. Her feet pounded and her heart sang as she and the other kids welcomed the spirits of their ancestors. They called out loudly and with great conviction as their heartbeats matched the beating of the drums. Their dancing lasted over an hour as their voices echoed through the forest and into the heavens.

Only after their legs seemed ready to collapse and their voices turned to squeaks did the Sachem appear. His stern face bared a hint of amusement, as his eyes seemed to smile. He seemed to favor this child because her laughter was almost contagious, even to him. The festivities continued as he approached the tribal fire. He stood there with his arms crossed as he gazed at the children dancing. "The ancestors would be pleased," he thought to himself.

He held his hands up to the heavens and shouted with great authority, "Manitou, may you look kindly upon the spirits of the children and protect them through life!" His voice rang out loudly, and everyone stood still as he spoke to the Great One. Weenuk was greatly respected by all tribes. Even rival warriors would give their lives for his safety, for without a spiritual leader a tribe was destined to perish.

All attention was focused on him as he lifted the small bowl and held it to the heavens. "Oh Manitou, Great Spirit, Master of the Universe, and Keeper of All Knowledge, I call upon you this day. Before me is this child that has been called Sheeta. She has passed seven years and has given honor to her name. It is time for her to shed her infant name and thoughts. She has earned the privilege to receive a name of youth. From this day forth she will be called Shena-hea (Child of the Spirits, in the language of the Stone People). All shall know this name and respect it for it is an honorable name."

After thinking about this special memory, Wishna-hea stretched out her arms in front of her and slipped beneath the surface of the water. She felt the refreshing freedom the waters afforded her. She dove deep into the river and headed for the water's edge. Her peaceful swim was suddenly interrupted by the noise of several horses stomping in the water. She hurled herself to the surface and her body filled with fear and excitement.

War cries filled the air as a raiding party, seven strong, charged through the water heading directly towards the sleeping village. They were the warriors of the Mohawk, the most treacherous of the Iroquois. Their bodies were painted and their hair stood on end like the quills of a porcupine. The sides of their scalps were plucked clean, which added to their fierce appearance.

Wishna-hea's eyes scanned the forest, for the Mohawks liked to attack from several directions at once. Seeing no other movements, her attention quickly snapped back to the charging raiders.

She stayed motionless in the water with only her head visible. Three warriors charged towards her and their horses' eyes glazed with excitement. Like the flash of a trout, her naked body broke the surface of the water and she vanished below. Even with her quickness and agility, she was no match for the horses that carried her attackers. Frantically, her legs and arms propelled her through the cold water. She never swam so strongly, still their hooves grew closer and closer. She fought forcefully to reach deep water so that she could slow down the horses. Unfortunately, the direction she was heading in only became shallower.

Her left foot brushed against a horse's leg, but before she could react, her head seemed to explode as a war club grazed the right side of it. Darkness swallowed her like a giant fish. As quickly as the pain came, it left, and in its place was nothing. There was no Great Spirit, no ancestors, no pristine creatures of the forest. There was only total darkness.

Slowly, like a storm filled morning, the darkness faded as she became aware of horseflesh beneath her naked stomach. The horse's whither dug into her flesh as she began to gain consciousness. Abruptly, she snapped her body up to try to free herself from her captor, but a strong hand forced her back against the horse. Suddenly, she was aware of her vulnerability and her nakedness. With a swift and solid movement she fought frantically to free herself from the horse and her captor. Again her face absorbed the impact of a strong fist, and from a vast distance she heard the words, "She lives, after all!" And again, the darkness enveloped her.

The horses' strides were great and the movements were as if she was gliding through the air. Wishna-hea was suspended between two worlds—the land of the living and the land of her ancestors. When in the land of the living, the only movement she was able to achieve was to lift her head slightly and view the blood-covered hair of the horse's side. Her head pounded and she was able to move her hand to the pain's source. The blood's warmth and stickiness told her of her capture, then darkness returned and she drifted closer to her ancestors.

When in the land of her ancestors, the pain had vanished and she felt as if she was soaring among the clouds, high above the treetops. She became aware of the sounds of the wind whistling in her ears, nearly as pleasant as a river trickling over rocks. The whooshing sounds of a great bird's wings echoed in the background.

Abruptly the pain returned with a ferocity that rippled through her body. A sharp pain radiated from her behind and snapped her back to the land of the living. Her captor's hand slapped viciously against her naked flesh again.

"Don't you die yet! You haven't felt my manhood," said a strange voice, as it echoed between the sounds of the horses' pounding hooves. Her head bounced loosely against the charging steed's shoulders. She tried to open her eyes, but they would not obey. Again she tried to free herself, but her body would not comply.

*"You shall not join your ancestors today. For I have been sent to protect you and give you my strength!"* The words did not enter her ears, but stayed in her mind. She understood their meaning and source. She saw the head of a mighty Eagle beneath her, as she soared upon deep slumber.

*"I angrily soared high above the bush, and locked my sight on the raiding party. I screeched noisily to summon Manitou and tell him of this deed. I asked for permission to attack. Manitou, in his infinite wisdom, granted me permission to kill all but the three who had taken Weenuk's woman, for he had better plans for them than mere death. I dove at the lead rider with a vengeance! I flexed my talons and locked my sight on the riders below. I called out to the other eagles for help."*

*"With the speed of lightning, I dropped from the sky. The braves in the back of the raiding party saw the attack coming, but were unable to warn the leader before my mighty talons struck. I dug deeply into the flesh of his shoulders and with two flaps of my wings I lifted him from his mount. I heard the others screaming as I thrust my powerful beak and snapped his neck like a twig. The other eagles soon joined in, and before the riders could reach the safety of the dense bush, they struck with nearly as much vengeance as I had. In no time at all, the other two riders quickly perished."*

Wishna-hea's limp body stayed pressed to the flesh of the horse and remained calm in her deep sleep. The horses charged through the bush and followed the trail leading to Eau Claire Gorge. Their mouths were frothing and their eyes were wild as they raced deeper and deeper into the forest. Unaware that the largest and most ferocious of the woodland animals waited in ambush, the unsuspecting riders charged on.

The mighty bear dug his claws deep into the bark of the tree and sharpened them. He then waited behind the mammoth rock and paced anxiously. He had chosen the place where the path narrowed—adjacent to the boulder were the walls of the Clear Waters dropped off sharply ten to twelve feet. After attacking a few horses, the bear allowed three warriors, the ones responsible for Wishna-hea's capture, to escape. Their punishment would be much more severe, and it had to be carried out by Him.

# Chapter 2

In her dreams, Wishna-hea witnessed a bloody battle between eagles and men; a huge bear and horses. The battle was bloody and carried out swiftly and decisively.

At first she was aware of her head bouncing. "I must be still on the horse," she thought, for her hips were raised higher than her head. Then she felt a muscle deep within her. "Weenuk must have come and rescued me."

Her man was behind her and thrusting inside of her roughly. His massive hands dug deeply into the flesh of her hips. "Weenuk has much hunger." A smile came over her lips as she moved her hips to greet his thrusts. It felt good, as did the warmth of his body on top of her. She kept her eyes closed and her head turned. Her legs spread wide and pressed deeply into the soft ground.

Something was different. She tried to focus her thoughts, but waves of darkness washed back over her mind. Urgency was beginning to creep up on her as both of their tempos increased. She was drifting once again between two lands . . . but something was definitely wrong!

At once the darkness vanished and her senses returned to her. She tried to open her eyes, but they were still so heavy. Her movements stopped, yet the pounding persisted. She could only see the ground beneath her face, and she struggled to move her head.

When her eyes came into focus, she couldn't believe what she saw. She tried to scream. She tried to struggle against the strong arms that held her down. It wasn't just one of those awful warriors, it was three of them. Two held her legs spread, while the third was deep inside her.

Her senses were now heightened and her strength was starting to return. "You dog," she screamed as her hands reached out to her sides seeking a weapon to use against her attacker.

"I will kill you!" she growled like an enraged bear. "Weenuk, kill him now!"

"The squaw hollers the name of the stupid old man, like he can help her now!" The warrior squeaked out as he continued to thrust into her.

"I am his woman, and he shall strike you dead!" she screamed at the top of her lungs.

As if a club hit him, her attacker jumped to his knees and quickly to his feet. With lightning speed she also sprung to her feet and grabbed a knife from one of their waistbands and lashed out with a vicious lunge. Sunak, one of the warriors, snatched her arm before she could come close to any of them.

"Woman, if you had been on my horse, I would have sliced your throat long ago. Don't try my patience!" he snarled as he bent her wrist back and forced her to her knees.

She bellowed, "I am Weenuk's woman and he shall hunt you down and kill you like snakes!"

All three looked at her and almost froze in their tracks. They thought back to the carnage they had witnessed, and it all started to make sense. Had they truly angered the Great Spirit? Was it His wrath they had encountered? Surely no other explanation could match the bazaar battle between man and beast.

Lachta's first reaction was to grab his knife and slit her throat, but he knew that his people would perish if he acted on that instinct. He looked down at the woman kneeling before him. He knew that the Mohawks were in grave danger. They must ride quickly to their hidden encampment and warn the others. He said, "Grab the woman. We have work to be done!"

The three men looked down at Wishna-hea. Her fiery eyes glared at them. She remained on her knees in defiance. None of them dared touch her.

Her strength was returning quickly, and she was starting to understand the power that kept her alive. "You shall all die at the hands of Manitou!"

Still frozen in their tracks they realized the truthfulness of her statement. Even her nakedness no longer seemed to register in their minds.

Lachta, sitting upon his horse, snapped out an order and regained their attention. "Hand the woman up to me!"

The two looked at her, but couldn't bring themselves to touch her. Lachta screamed out, "You fools! She is just a woman; she will not hurt you. She is mere flesh and blood, and if you do not hurry, I shall be the one killing you both!"

Realizing they still were not moving, he roared, "Now!"

The two of them looked at Wishna-hea, and in an almost apologetic manner, held out their hands to help her up. She took both of their hands and pulled herself to a standing position. Her head spun a bit at the quickness of the moment, but it soon cleared.

She glared at Lachta as he held his hand down to her. She totally disapproved of his decision to have her sit upon his horse with him.

"I have no time for your foolishness, woman!" he barked at her. "You can barely stand, and we must ride quickly."

Begrudgingly, she jumped onto the horse and quipped, "Touch me, and you die!"

Wishna-hea thought of diving from the horse's back many times, but realized that it would mean her death, not from the waters but from her captors. The words of the Eagle continued to echo in her mind. *"You shall not join your ancestors today. I have been sent to watch over you, and give you my strength."*

When word of Wishna-hea's capture spread through the forest, warriors from several tribes assembled and began to comb the forests. With intensity for revenge, they scoured the woods for any signs of the Mohawk dogs. When tracks were discovered leading to the water, they gathered on each side of the river and began to search the riverbanks for signs of their enemy. Their eyes and ears scanned the forest and all of its creatures. The tracks of the Mohawk's horses revealed three horses with four riders. One walked with shoulders heavy, revealing two riders on one horse, and the depth of the prints indicated the second person was lighter.

Wishna-hea knew the warriors would be scouring the forest for them, and it was just a matter of time before they rescued her. She remained calm and focused. While her captors watched the forests and the river, her eyes scanned the sky. She knew her protector would be watching, and her eyes searched desperately for some reassurance.

Lachta's eyes scanned the forest and the banks of the river. He looked for a place to leave the river's turbulence. The horses moved slowly, and distance was their best ally, but they would have to find a place where there was solid rock to leave the waters behind them. The horses' hoof prints would not show on the stone, and the water from their mounts would dry quickly on the warmed rocks.

They traveled for more than a mile down the river searching desperately for a place to exit the water. The horses were getting tired. Sunak's eyes snapped to attention when his horse's ear perked up and pointed to the left side of the bank. He raised his arm straight up, signaling the others to stop immediately. They all quickly scanned the banks and the bush. They froze in their tracks, and Wishna-hea smiled, because she knew her freedom would soon be at hand.

Lachta was the first to spot the deer, which was nearly concealed among the dense undergrowth that lined the banks of the river. He scanned the area, looking for the safest place to leave the river. Cautiously they approached the bank. Sunak lead the way, with the sound of his beating heart nearly blanketing the sounds of the river and bush. Only after he was totally satisfied that the spot was safe, did he signal the others to come ashore.

The forest was crawling with more than a hundred warriors from numerous villages of the Algonquin. Old acquaintances were renewed as warriors from the many villages were once again united with bloodlust in their hearts. The Mohawks would be ferreted out and destroyed from their lands, and once again, peace would be re-established.

Faith keepers of all the villages and tribes called out to Manitou, pleading for His help in recovering Wishna-hea. The Blackfoot, the Mississauga, the Cree, and the Micmacks were the first to respond and send out scouting parties to hunt and destroy any and all Mohawk warriors from their lands. The respect the Montagnais earned from the other tribes was just, for their leaders were wise and their warriors fierce.

With a sigh of relief, the three Mohawks dismounted and held the muzzle of their horses to quiet them. The bush was all too quiet. Neither a bird nor a squirrel could be heard. Even Wishna-hea sat upon the ground listening silently for any sounds. The horses stood frozen. Their keen eyes and ears searched the land for any signs of danger. Still nothing was heard nor seen.

The clearing was large enough to allow them room to move and defend themselves if attacked, but still offered a safe haven from observation. Wishna-hea's eyes scanned the treetops. The towering white pines totally obscured the vision of even the Eagle, she thought to herself. The total silence was even unnerving to her as she sat motionless, listening and watching.

Sumac was the first to react to a faint sound. His ears perked up, and he raised his right hand to signal the others. Even the horses picked up on his signals. They began to turn and twist, looking for the source of danger.

"Surely, you do not fear this old man!" A voice echoed in the air.

Wishna-hea's heart leaped as she recognized the voice instantly, she stood quickly, and a broad smile covered her face. The heads and minds of the others turned and twisted in all directions looking for the source, ready to strike out. A ray of sunlight broke through the boughs of the pines and out of thin air appeared an old man sitting on the ground with his legs crossed and his hands at his sides.

"Strike not, this old man, I have no fear of your arrows or war club. You shall only anger me!"

A look of utter disbelief covered all of their faces. Where did he come from, and why is he not afraid?

"I am Weenuk!" After a short pause, he continued, "Which of you has taken my woman from me?" His voice boomed and his eyes stabbed fiercely.

Even Wishna-hea sat frozen in time and space. While her reaction was from amazement, theirs was from total fear. Weenuk's image intensified and grew larger than life, blocking the bush behind him.

"Speak!" His command echoed through the wilderness like the sound of thunder.

Sumac's hand instinctively went to draw back the string of his bow, and instantaneously a bolt of lightning shot from the eyes of Weenuk and struck him dead. A second bolt shot out and ended the life of the third Mohawk, who had been standing helplessly with his hands at his sides.

Lachta stood with eyes agape and his hands frozen on his bow, unable to move.

"You are wise to be afraid, Lachta, for you have angered even Manitou!" The man's voice echoed. "You have taken my woman, and dishonored her. For this you shall die, and your people as well! Your warriors have raided our villages, killed our warriors, stolen our horses, and we allowed you to survive. Now you have chosen a path to destruction, and Manitou's vengeance shall rein over your lands and rid your people from here, forever!"

"I did not know I had taken the woman of Weenuk, until long after we left your village!" Lachta spoke in his defense.

"Did you not know of this while you dishonored her?" Weenuk's voice intensified.

"No, Weenuk! I did not know of this until after. I swear to you on my honor!"

A great roar, greater than the strongest thunder boomed throughout the lands of the Algonquin, and fear swept through everyone's soul. Even the horses and animals of the wilderness felt the fear and power that had been unleashed.

Terror entered Lachta as the claw of the greatest bear the North had ever known swung down, impaling his body and lifting him high in the air. His lifeless body was limp, while his eyes stared straight into the mighty bear's fangs.

Wishna-hea stood frozen in total astonishment as she watched this enormous bear, whose knees stood higher than her body, torturing his prey. Lachta's life ended when the bear's huge teeth crushed his neck and snapped his head from his rag-like body.

Wishna-hea watched in horror as the headless body dropped to the ground. In an instant, the Bear vanished into thin air. After breaking her trance, she turned quickly to see Weenuk. Yet, he, too, had vanished, leaving behind only the blanket that she had slept under for many years.

She knelt on the ground, tears streaming from her eyes. Now she became aware of her nakedness and looked down at her body in shame. She picked up the blanket and wrapped it tightly around her shivering body.

# Chapter 3

Knowing the importance of retrieving the headless torso, Wishna-hea struggled with Lachta's body. The slickness from his blood made it nearly impossible to lift him onto the horse. Even the horse resisted, and would not stand still.

Abandoning her attempts to lift the body, she instead propped him forward and hooked her arms under his armpits, so she could lift, as well as drag the torso to the bank of the river. The stench and sight of the mutilated body beneath her chin nearly nauseated her, but she held her breath and closed her eyes and lifted with all her might. The lifeless body proved to be more than she could handle. No matter how much she tried she could not drag it more than a few feet.

She glanced down and a shriek escaped from deep within her. Her naked body was now totally covered with blood. Frantically, she tried to wipe the blood away with her hands, but they, too, were now covered with warm blood. Panic filled her eyes and she raced to the river. She must cleanse herself.

She stumbled through the shallow waters to the center of the river. Dropping to her knees, she fell forward and allowed the water to envelop her. The river diluted her salty tears. Her enemy's blood was rinsed from her flesh. The waters soothed her, and washed away the blood. She lay there for several moments, allowing the water to comfort her once again. Slowly she rose to her knees, and then turned to face the river's flow.

"Oh, Manitou, I have witnessed your fury and rage. You have

made yourself visible and protected me from harm and I must dedicate my life to you. Naho."

Once again, she knelt in the fast moving water and closed her eyes, opening her mind. She sensed Manitou's smile, for he knew of her gratitude. A wave of anxiety swept over her and once again her eyes filled with tears and her heart filled with repulsion at the thought of her captor's blood on her body. With the sand from the river's base she frantically scrubbed and rinsed, rinsed and scrubbed until her flesh was nearly raw. The tears streamed down her cheeks and trickled into the waters of the Eau Claire.

When she had no strength left, she collapsed on the bank. She rolled onto her side, curled into a ball, and sobbed. Her sobs lasted a long time, for her heart ached and her memory burned.

When she had finally regained her strength, she took the blanket that Weenuk had left for her, grabbed a knife from one of the man's waistbands, and created a cloak for herself.

It wasn't long before word of Wishna-hea's ordeal spread throughout the bush. She was soon joined by people from her village, as well as warriors from surrounding villages.

As was custom, Wishna-hea was given her choice of horses to ride, since all three horses now belonged to her. She chose a horse, and a few warriors from her village lifted the three tattered bodies onto the remaining two horses. During the return voyage, additional warriors joined the procession. As they did, they not only noticed her trophy horses, but they also noticed the headless body of one of the men. How had this woman so brutally slain her captors? When they asked her this question, she simply told them that she would tell them the entire story when she arrived safely at her village.

Her brother took the lead with Wishna-hea. Through silent communication, their sibling love was passed between them. The trails were only wide enough to allow two riders abreast, so the procession wound its way through the trails of the wilderness.

The giant white pines towered above them and the birds sang, and the animals of the wilderness watched silently.

The journey lasted nearly three hours. Weenuk had already told the tribe members that she was safe and would be returning soon. They were all anxious to see her. However, none of them had any idea about how she was saved in the forest.

At the first sign of the returning tribe members, the entire village sprang to life. The women ran to welcome Wishna-hea back. The children ran to see why there was so much excitement, and the rest of the village just wanted to be part of the homecoming. Wishna-hea was not only Weenuk's woman, but she was also the most important woman of the village.

The procession paraded around the entire village, with each horse prancing proudly, before ending up at Weenuk's lodge. He walked out proudly and held his arms up to Manitou in thanks. He beamed with pride and knew that Manitou had chosen his village, and more specifically, his woman, to lead his people into the future.

Wishna-hea slid off her horse and took Weenuk's hands in hers. Their spirits had bonded and she now understood the power of her man. Manitou had allowed Weenuk to exercise such powers in order to allow his woman's safe return. Now she, too, would be able to speak to Manitou and her thoughts would be understood. She was now bonded to Him for the rest of eternity. Together the reunited couple looked into each other's eyes and looked far beyond.

The respect for Weenuk grew. The Montagnais were now the most feared warriors in the land. The spectacle in front of them gave living proof of what happens to those who dare to challenge the laws of Manitou.

The tribal fire grew as many logs were placed upon it. The women cooked many dishes on the smaller fire as the festivities proceeded. The warriors, who first came upon Wishna-hea in the woods, were the first to be allowed to dance in front of the tribal fire. Their chanting echoed through out the heavens; calling the attention of their ancestors. For it was said that the spirits could no longer understand the words of man, but watched their dancing intently.

The dancers told of the bodies that were found upon the ground, and the huge footprints of the mighty bear. They told of the brave woman who sat upon the horse of her captor. They then told of the headless corpse. Everyone's eyes and imaginations were fixed upon the dancers and all were filled with the sense of awe.

While they danced, Wishna-hea remained in her lodge, for it was not permissible for her to hear or see the accounts of the others. Her dance was not to be influenced by the other's stories. After several hours of dancers and festivities, it was finally Wishna-hea's time to tell her story.

She wore a dress that was made by her mother. It had turquoise and white beads on the front, which symbolized her newfound importance. Her hair draped down to her waist and was braided and tied with colorful beads. Her beauty was only surpassed by her importance to her people.

She walked slowly from her lodge with Weenuk at her side. The boisterous crowd of spectators became silent as she approached the fire. Weenuk held his hands up to the Heavens and in his loudest voice announced, "Manitou, I present to you and to all of those who have gathered in our village, the woman who has been selected by you to be the messenger of your teachings. May her dance be acceptable to you."

With that introduction, Wishna-hea stepped forward and the drums began to beat. She began by holding her hands up high to the East, to tell of the morning sun's arrival, and all were engrossed by her dance. Her arms moved fluidly in the gestures of swimming and she began to twirl as if suspended by the water's buoyancy. Her dance was slow and rhythmic, and the drummer kept pace with her movements.

She stopped abruptly and raised her hands above her eyebrows. Everyone knew what was coming next, but they waited to hear her version of the story. Her head snapped abruptly to the side, and a gasp was heard from the crowd. Her head rolled and twisted around and around. Her dancing spoke of her forcible rape, and everyone gasped and filled with rage. She told of the power Weenuk's name held to her captors, and everyone was infused with pride and joy. Her antics displayed her defiance towards her captors and their subsequent ride to flee those who searched for her. The sounds of countless gasps of breath broke their silence as she began telling of the events that lead to her miraculous salvation.

She held her hands up to her eyes and snapped them open to show the lightning bolts that shot from Weenuk's eyes. The light and shadows from the fire only added to the suspense of her dance. When she began to tell of Weenuk's transformation into the greatest of Bears, everyone gasped in total amazement. Their eyes fixed on her and then on Weenuk. Manitou himself had granted their Spiritual Leader tremendous power.

Before their very eyes, her image seemed to grow. All the dancers before her told of the deafening roar that was heard above the forest's highest trees, but none was prepared for her description of its source.

Every person there sat and watched in total amazement. Even the infants watched carefully, mesmerized by her story. When her story was finished, everyone chanted and shouted loudly to the ancestors, signifying their approval of her description of the events.

The corpses were displayed. Lachta's body was raised higher than the others for his courage was greater. Even though they were the enemy, all understood the importance of bravery and gave it respect.

Throughout the night and well into the next day, the sounds of their merriment were heard throughout the wilderness. Peace once again prevailed. During the next two days and nights, Wishna-hea and Weenuk spent many hours in each other's arms. A warmth and deep seeded love passed between them. Never were their bonds so strong. When they slept she pressed her body against his and allowed the love and respect to pass freely between them.

When the moon had risen to the top of the heavens on the second night, Weenuk spoke to Wishna-hea, "Woman, I have grieved because of your capture." His voice was soft, "Because of this, I summoned the Great Spirit and told him of my sorrow. He spoke of your safe return and that I must give to you a symbol of my love." With that he drew the knife from his belt and handed it to her.

"Take this and hold it against my finger," he said as he placed his left hand flat upon the robe which lay upon the ground.

"But I am not worthy," she said. "And I need no other symbols of the strength of our love for each other, for I know the feelings in our hearts."

"Speak no more of this, for I vowed my love."

"But I . . . ."

Before she could continue, he demanded her obedience. "Hold the knife and speak no more!"

Obeying his wishes, she held the knife against his small finger. With a clenched fist he slammed down upon the back of the blade, and like a twig, his finger snapped off. Only a trickle of blood escaped from the injured hand, for as a Sachem, he had total control of his body. With his right hand he picked up the severed finger and placed it in a medicine pouch and hung it from her neck.

"This, my woman, I present to you, for you are truly a part of me."

Wishna-hea held the pouch to her breast, and a tear trickled down her cheek. The magnitude of the events from the past two days finally struck her and the emotions that she hid could no longer be contained. Tears streamed down her cheeks and she placed her head in Weenuk's lap. Her body trembled and she cried in silence. Weenuk placed his hand upon her shoulders and a tear trickled down his weathered and aged cheek, as well. It would not be wise for others to see his weakness for they would question his strength, but in the presence of Wishna-hea, there were no secrets. The pain in her heart and head were shared with him, and he was glad for the oneness.

"Come, my woman, and dry your eyes, for today there is much celebrating!"

The dancing lasted long into the second night, and even the children were allowed to witness the re-enactments of bravery, for bravery and honesty were the ways of their people.

There was an endless stream of visitors to the village, because everyone wanted to see the power of Manitou and Weenuk. Each new arrival stood before the headless torso and gazed at the size of the wounds inflicted by the claws of the Great One. Instinctively, they looked at their clenched fists and realized the claws were thicker than any man's fist.

By the second day, the last of the sachems arrived to speak to Weenuk. Each would bring their finest horse as a gift in exchange for his wisdom. His powers would be spoken of forever, and by learning from him, their own powers would escalate. Their strength would dominate their enemies and peace would prevail. The village became prosperous. Old friendships were strengthened and new ones were made.

On the height of the moon of the third night, the Mohawks' bodies were burned on a pyre, so their spirits could be released. The evening was solemn, and the visiting friends all gathered. Few words were spoken. The three pyres were built and wood was stacked to within a foot of the three corpses. A ceremony like this had never been performed for an enemy before, but the Mohawks had tested the powers of both Weenuk and Manitou, and they had died brave and proud.

The drums began and the rattles were heard. Weenuk exited his lodge and walked deliberately to stand in front of the pyres. A torch was held high in his right hand. He looked out at those who had gathered and stood with his arms raised to the heavens. The drumbeats stopped so everyone could hear his words.

"Oh, Manitou, in your great wisdom, you have taken the lives of these Mohawk Dogs, but it is now time to return their spirits back to their ancestors. Let their people know we are just and all powerful. Our lands will be held sacred to those who oppose us, and a welcome place for those who are our friends. Let it be known that Weenuk wants peace among all our brothers. Let the elders of the villages speak of this to their young, and let them also learn of this. Manitou, let the battles of war be ended and let our people prosper. Naho!"

He turned and faced the pyres and lowered the torch to the kindling, and within moments the raging inferno signaled to the ancestors of the Mohawks. The light from the flames leapt high into the sky, and when the flames were at their highest, the souls of the Mohawks rose and traveled to the lands of their ancestors. When the bodies tumbled into the center of the fire, a stench filled the air, but no one dared to turn away. They watched until the flames were gone and only the embers remained.

# Chapter 4

Life soon returned to normal and the people of the village got on with their lives. The moon of the tall grass would soon be upon them, and there were many preparations to be made. The planting season was by far the busiest time of the year.

Weenuk was now the wealthiest of the tribe and had many horses. He planned to sell many of them to the horse trader near Trout Lake, then go to the Hudson Bay Trading Post to get many things to make their lives easier. Normally he would avoid going to the trading post, because the missionaries who lived nearby would swarm around him, figuring he was a prized package. They occasionally came to the village, and he soon learned they could be even more bothersome than the black flies in the growing season.

The white men had such an offensive smell. They barely understood the language of his people, but would incessantly tell of a better God—one that wasn't good enough to walk the lands himself and had to send a son to walk as a man. When word came that the missionaries were approaching the village, Weenuk would often discover an urgent matter that would take him far from their presence. Weenuk was always considered a prize to them, so he made himself harder to find than a mosquito in the seasons of snow.

Wishna-hea's life changed overnight, but gradually she grew familiar with her new ways. Her popularity among the other women increased ten-fold. She was now sought whenever any activities were taking place.

The women of her tribe were highly respected and treated well. Many even sat upon the tribal council. They were chosen for their wisdom and their ability to see into the future. Wishna-hea had a seat of high honor on the council. She sat on the left side of Weenuk. On his right was Chief Amable du Fond. Since Wishna-hea's experiences, the council met frequently. There were many things to discuss, and the little girl that once amused all of the elders with her smiles and playful antics was now the council's most important speaker.

Since her experience with the Great Bear, Wishna-hea's opinions were highly revered, and the others would sit and listen to her thoughts without interruption. It was felt that her thoughts on matters reflected not only her wisdom, but also her love for all of her people. Her views were often from the heart, as well as the mind. Even Weenuk encouraged her to tell the council more of her thoughts. The members often differed in their views, but all views were listened to and considered.

Wishna-hea now went to the river to swim with the other women, but still remained closely guarded at all times. She was no longer allowed to swim beneath the surface of the water alone. Her friendship with the fishes faded into memory.

Her time was now occupied by many different things. She was called into Weenuk's lodge whenever traveling dignitaries visited. They wanted to meet the woman who had changed the history of her people. She told the story of her release each time a new visitor arrived. They asked her many questions, and each time she spoke, Weenuk would sit silently watching, not only Wishna-hea, but also the visitor.

Not since Champlain and his soldiers had stayed with the Nipissing for the winter to defend their lands against the Iroquois, had such a display of power been witnessed. Champlain often referred to the Nipissing as the Sorcerers. Now the powers of the Montagnais surpassed their sister tribe. Their teachings were sought after by all of the tribes.

It was often spoken that when Weenuk traveled to the land of their ancestors, Wishna-hea would assume his place in the tribe.

Her wisdom was growing rapidly. She spent many hours each day with Weenuk in a smoke filled lodge learning his craft. She was now allowed travel to the Waterfall of Manitou, and heard some of the conversations Weenuk and Manitou carried on. Soon, she would be allowed into the lodge of Manitou, but she still had much knowledge to learn.

One morning she walked to the river and enjoyed feeling the sun's powerful rays on her face. Her guard's observant eyes watched carefully over her and the surrounding areas. She looked to the sky and smiled. The Eagle's massive wings spread out wide and the air rushed under them and kept him high aloft. Soaring in huge circles, she knew that his eyes were upon her as she sat upon a rock on the river's edge. The birds of the bush sang merrily and once again, she was at peace. The river welcomed her. The babbling of the water over the rocks was soothing to her ears, and the gentle breeze felt cool and refreshing against her face.

She felt the energy from the river surging into her body, and it revitalized her spirit. The fears that had become part of her were dissipating rapidly. Once again she felt at home in her surroundings. Perhaps soon she would feel the urge to swim again with the fishes, but on this day she just enjoyed the power she gained from the water and the forest around her. She breathed in deeply and smelled the clean crisp aroma of the pines, and filled her lungs with their fragrances. Once again, all was well.

From a distance she could hear the shouts and laughter from many of the braves that were deeply engrossed in a game of lacrosse. While the other women of the tribe did their work, the men enjoyed the competition of the game. She walked over to join the spectators. This was a good time for all. The wagers on the game were small because it was early in the season. However, by the time the leaves changed colors, the wagers would be significantly higher. Now they all played for the fun of the game and the action was light hearted.

The score was two-one and the players were engrossed in the game. There were often visitors from other tribes who would test their skills against her tribe's players. She watched intently, while chatting with several others about which side she favored, and humorously exchanged comments about each of the players. Shouts of encouragement echoed through the forests, and the scoring of another point brought all the spectators to their feet.

The game lasted several hours, and the crowd changed frequently. Chores still had to be done, and by listening to the shouts of those watching, it was easy to understand what was going on with the game, even from a distance.

Wishna-hea learned most of the curative plants Weenuk used and she would take frequent walks deep into the bush to retrieve them. She often enjoyed the company of the men that were chosen to guard her. It was considered an honor to be one of her guards, and they all looked forward to talking to her in private conversations. Her questions were sincere, and all conversations were always spoken in confidence. They respected her, not only as Weenuk's woman, but also as a close friend.

Many thought that she had the powers to actually call the animals of the forest. It seemed that when she went into the bush her guards saw more game than usual, though she forbade them from killing animals while they escorted her on her walks. She told them that she promised the animals safety, for they had greatly aided in her defense. The animals understood this, and they, too, would come to see the Queen of the Montagnais.

At first, her guards would automatically raise their weapons when seeing a deer or animal large enough to share at mealtime. However, her sharp words reminded them of her wishes and the guards reluctantly lowered their weapons. Instead, they were forced to watch the animals enjoying their leisure. As a result, their understanding of the animals' ways was increased, and they became better prepared for hunting.

When she walked away from her guards, she always used a walking stick. When teased about being afraid of perhaps a snake, she explained her reasoning—man is the only animal in Manitou's kingdom that walks only on two legs, all other creatures use all four. When the animals hear only two feet walking, they instinctively know it is man, and are fearful for their lives. When they hear a third foot, their inquisitive nature gets the best of them, and they must look for its source.

This simple lesson added greatly to her guards' hunting successes. Despite the fact that she carried no weapon, except a sharp knife, they learned as much from her as from any man they had ever known. She taught them to observe the ways of an animal and understand its soul.

The guards never let on the new insights they learned, nor its source. The other hunters were often amazed by their repeated successes, and when asked, they would shrug their shoulders and simply walk away, secretly smiling to themselves. Only when they were alone with her other guards would they share ideas.

That night, Wishna-hea lay under the stars, staring up at the heavens. The light from the innumerable stars cut their way through the pitch-black sky. Her spirit freed itself from its earthly bonds and began to float high above her body, and soon joined the twinkling stars. The air was warm, and the cool gentle breeze welcomed her. She floated aimlessly, searching the heavens for her favorite star.

It was believed that each star was the soul of an ancestor, and the brighter the star, the more important the ancestor was when he or she walked the Earth. During her weightless flight, Wishna-hea heard a sound that was not of man's world, but of the spirit world. It whispered, "You are favored, among all women of the lands, but there is change in the winds. You will accept these changes and use them to teach the others of things which must be learned."

In the corner of her eye she saw a man change into an owl and then fly away in silence. Her earthly form neither turned its head nor altered its focus on the distant star. She lay there for a long time in quiet contemplation. She wanted to tell Weenuk of her vision, but wanted to gain a clear understanding of it before she shared it with him. Her spirit rejoined her earthly form, and she continued laying in silence, searching for the answer. Nothing came to her. Aware that she would not find the answer by herself, she stood up and walked to her lodge in silence.

Weenuk's words startled her as he stood patiently just outside the lodge. "Woman, we have shared an important vision. Come now, and we shall speak of this."

His words were soft and comforting. They walked into their lodge and sat upon the ground as the flickering flames of the small fire broke through the darkness. The light reflected off their bodies, and his expression revealed the graveness of his thoughts.

The hours passed slowly as they discussed the possible meaning of the vision. The night lingered on, and finally it was decided that they must sleep on it. Perhaps their dreams would lend a clearer understanding, but sleep came slowly.

The next few days passed uneventfully. Both Weenuk and Wishna-hea shared a solemn attitude, but neither spoke to the other members of the council about this. They had to discover its meanings, and neither of them could gain an understanding. Finally after the third day, a tribal council meeting was called.

Weenuk began, "Wishna-hea and I have shared a vision, which has troubled both of us. I have asked Manitou of its meaning, and He has given me no replies." He continued to explain the vision they both shared, and asked the other members if they knew of any events that may possibly have caused the vision. To his dismay, none of them had any input. He told the others that they would plan future meetings and asked them to find out if other tribe members had witnessed anything out of the ordinary.

Another week passed and no insights were gained. The anticipation of a memorable event hung over everyone's heads like a giant cloud. All of the tribal elders kept a watchful eye, and riders were sent out to seek the counsel of other tribes to see if they had any information. Unfortunately, nothing was uncovered. Rumors were beginning to spread through the village, and everyone was jumping to conclusions about what the changes in the wind could possibly be. As with all rumors, they soon faded in the wind. However, the increasing presence of men who cut down trees like beavers in their area worried them slightly, but didn't raise enough concerns to merit serious discussion.

During this time, Wishna-hea started having stomach sickness in the mornings. Her remedies usually dispelled any sickness, but this particular stomach malady kept recurring. She casually mentioned her queasy stomach to Weenuk, but did not tell him of its frequency, nor had she mentioned it to the other women of the village.

That is until the morning when one of the other women of the village heard her emptying her stomach. Before she knew it, everyone in the village was buzzing with excitement. Wishna-hea would soon become a mother, and her offspring would be of great importance to her people. A great celebration was planned and riders were sent to the other villages to announce the event.

The celebration started early and lasted for days. She had no idea that so many people would come to honor her anticipated birth. When, however, a person is so favored by Manitou, only good things can stem from it. It had been told in both of their visions. The child would live a long life and teach the lessons of its parents to the others, long after they both had perished.

Wishna-hea felt nervous about all the fuss that everyone was making. It was common among her people to have their babies pass into the lands of their ancestors before they had seen their second winter. Names would not be given before that time. It was felt that it was easier to part with one that had no name. She spoke of her reluctance to Weenuk and he reminded her of their shared vision.

"Our people must celebrate this, for Manitou has blessed you, and will watch over you."

The women prepared many of their favorite dishes, and the men brought several deer back to the village. It appeared that even the bush made its donations to this joyous occasion.

The women made a special deerskin dress for Wishna-hea, which left plenty of room for growth in her stomach and breast areas. The feathers of the Eagle and the Owl were sewn onto the front of the dress, since she was under the watchful eye of Manitou.

Some of the men perfected a new dance, and they meditated deeply before performing it so they could gain inspiration to make the dance more meaningful. They performed it on the cliff of Clear Waters Gorge, where the sounds of the bush were drowned out by the rage of the waters. They stayed there for countless hours, with their minds cleansed of all worldly matters.

Members from other villages began arriving, and many of them brought young horses for the unborn child. By the time the child was old enough to ride, the horses would be ready to bear the child's weight.

The women's most prized dishes were served throughout the days and nights. Laughter filled the air and everyone seemed very happy. Weenuk and Wishna-hea examined each new horse that arrived with great pleasure. Their herd of horses would soon become the talk of the lands, and each new horse that was given to them was even better than the last.

Wishna-hea welcomed so many visitors that her arms became weary from the traditional greetings. It was a time of great joy for all, but especially for her. When the celebration finally came to an end, she rested her body in Weenuk's arms and had another vision appear to her—only this time it was not happy. It was a dreadful vision, one that seemed so real and close.

# Chapter 5

The vision began with the headless Mohawk. His laughter echoed in her mind. He spoke in vile words and talked of things only Weenuk would ever be allowed to use in her presence. His laughter was loud and obnoxious. Though headless, his words came through very clearly. The laughter continued to grow louder and louder and more offensive.

When she woke up, she had tears streaming down her face and she was shaking. Weenuk was already awake, and he was laying with his eyes open, staring into the darkness. He, too, shared the vision. Had they misinterpreted their last vision?

"We must speak of this vision." His voice was cold and unyielding.

Unsure which was more frightening, the vision or the tone of Weenuk's voice, she said, "What is the meaning of this vision?"

"Perhaps it is not I who had planted the growth inside you!" His words stung.

Neither she nor Weenuk had given that a moment's thought before this vision. Her tears dried up instantly and she sat up and looked deeply into his eyes. Though they sat in near total darkness, his eyes still beamed at her, and she felt his intensity.

"What does this mean, Weenuk?" Her voice trembled.

His words cut like a knife. "I am not allowed to have a woman who carries another's seed, especially one of our enemy."

She sat and stared at him in disbelief. Her mouth agape and her heart crushed. A sob welled up inside her and she wanted to reach out to him. She wanted to have him hold her in his arms, yet he didn't move at all. He just sat there motionless and emotionless. She began to tremble uncontrollably. Though he could not see this, he felt it deeply, as if his heart had been wrenched from his chest. If true, he would never be able to hold the woman whom he loved so deeply or feel the warmth of her against him. He would never be able to listen or speak to her again.

They both sat in silence and didn't move until the dawn. Weenuk knew of the punishment that tradition demanded, and he dared not think of the devastating consequences. He did not want her to know of it, at least not yet.

As the light entered their lodge she could see the sadness and despair in his eyes. She had wept silently most of the night. She had done no wrong, yet the laws of their lands were harsh and decisive.

"When the sun is high we shall call the others to decide your fate." Weenuk spoke softly and the words came flatly from his lips.

"But Weenuk, I have done no wrong!" She sobbed softly. The words barely reached his ears.

He turned and walked to the door. His large shoulders slumped and his head down. He turned and said to her, "When I named you, Tadpole, I knew in my heart that I would always favor you. You have made my heart light. When you were captured, you brought out a rage that I have never felt before. If I would have known, I would have come to your side quicker and my revenge would have been swift. Now the Mohawk dog laughs at me, for he has taken my woman from me. He has done this in a way that is like a barb on a hook, and shall haunt me until I join my ancestors."

He stood completely still. He looked down at her as she knelt on the floor. Her eyes were swollen and red. Reluctantly, she looked up at him, and from her unspoken words, he knew that she would love him forever. She knew that his heart felt the same as hers. They remained motionless, their eyes locked on each other's.

"Come, my woman. We must tell the others and prepare ourselves." His words were barely more than a whisper. He held his massive hand out to her.

When she put her hand in his, Weenuk said, "Manitou spared you, knowing of this. I cannot question his wisdom. He was wise to take the head from that Mohawk dog, for I would have declared war on all the Iroquois, and there would have been a blood war that would have lasted until the last dog was slain. He was wise. I shall see that no harm comes to you, for you are guiltless, and your heart is true."

She rose up and wrapped her other hand around his and looked deep into his eyes. For a moment, the years were shed from his body, like the winter coat in spring. He stood before her as a young and fierce warrior, but soon the pain returned and he once again became an old and defeated man. They walked hand in hand.

They walked East to the home of Grandfather Sun. The sweat lodge, where this matter must be taken care of, was a short distance from the village. Tribal law stated that a woman of the sachem must remain pure, except if she carries his child. However, if she carries the seed of another man, her punishment is death.

No one in the village had ever imagined that Wishna-hea, a woman of such a high esteem, would ever be kidnapped and raped, but this was exactly what had happened. The tribal council had to vote on this very delicate situation.

Weenuk chanted over the small fire in the lodge, calling Manitou to their meeting. Everyone sat in a close circle around the fire, and their eyes gave a clear indication of their sorrow. Wishna-hea's hands were damp and her heart beat fast. She sat upon her legs and stared intently into the flames of the fire. Her concentration blocked out the others, even Weenuk.

The message from Manitou was unclear to any of the tribal council. Weenuk's chanting droned on and a drum beat steadily. Weenuk's voice and the drum both became louder. The aroma of the sweet grass filled the lodge and everyone's eyes were fixed on the fire's flames.

Soon the smoke obscured everyone's vision in the lodge. The droning continued and penetrated everyone's senses. Smoke filled their lungs and heightened their senses.

"Make your presence known, Great One, and let us know of your wisdom."

Weenuk spoke in the language of the Spirits, where thoughts became the only source of communication. Manitou chose not to enter the smoke—filled lodge; instead he brought the tribal council to him. This was easily accomplished, since his powers were so vast. He lifted their spirits from the lodge and brought them to a special place.

"We seek the wisdom of Manitou." Weenuk thought in his head. Manitou's presence was felt, and each tribal council member experienced His presence in his or her own unique way. Their communal thought strengthened their powers and they knew He was among them. They no longer felt the Earth beneath them, yet no one had moved a muscle.

The gentle winds brushed against them lightly, as they were propelled upward. Each member was reluctant to open his or her eyes. The exhilaration of flight heightened all of their senses. Higher and higher they traveled. Although they all knew that they traveled in unison, they still felt isolated.

Finally, one of the elders broke the spell and opened his eyes, gazing at the world beneath him. "Look," he shouted in his excitement.

With that, everyone snapped their eyes open and gazed at the Earth beneath them. The clouds looked like giant puffs of the softest snow, and the sky blazed in its brilliance. Never before had they imagined their world so beautiful, nor so much at peace. For most of them, they were given the opportunity to view the world from the perspective of the Sacred Eagle.

Suddenly loud noises filled the air. They could hear men shouting words they didn't understand. These men were dressed in the brightly colored furs of an animal they did not recognize. The air was thick and smelled foul. Fields went on nearly forever and the bush had been cut back. Even the tree roots had

disappeared. Trees that once stood tall now lay stacked in piles.
The men walked in and out of these piles. Rocks were piled high
against the stacked trees, and smoke escaped from the cracks.
The animals of the forest were timid and hid from sight. In fact,
they had all but disappeared completely.

At first, the tribal members thought the Iroquois had attacked
their lands and built these strange wonders. However, they soon
realized that it was these men who cut the trees like beavers. The
forests of the bush were opened in strange ways. Wide paths now
covered their lands. These paths went in straight lines and crossed
other paths over and over again. It seemed like the pathmakers
could no longer think and lost their reason. The paths were very
wide and offered no concealment. Had the enemy lost its capacity
to think?

Each of the elders looked at the lands beneath them, and
they knelt in order to gain a better view. Their eyes scanned a
distance farther than they could ride in several days. They knelt
in total silence and disbelief. They realized that there was not a
single member of their tribe anywhere. In fact, there were no
tribal people at all.

Graveness filled all of their eyes and their hearts were deeply
saddened. Is this the fate that is in front of us? Have all our
people joined their ancestors? All of them? There were no teepees.
There was no laughter from their children. There were no women
in the fields. There were horses, but they were contained by
strange strings with sharp edges and the limbs of trees.

Someone commented that everyone should look closely at
the horses. As they did, they quickly realized that the spirits of
the horses had been broken, and the fire in their eyes had been
extinguished.

The elders scanned desperately to find even a single sign of
their way of life. Slowly they each sat back upon their heels with
blank eyes. Tears streamed down the faces of two women, but no
one commented on their weakness. It wasn't long before others
joined in and tears poured like water from a waterfall. They all
sat silently in their sadness.

"What have you done to our people, Great One?" Anger filled Weenuk, and his words traveled faster than his mind. "We have followed your teachings, and have learned Your ways and those of our ancestors. Why have you destroyed our people?"

He raised his voice in challenge, which no man had ever done to Manitou. Yet the Great One allowed it to pass unheeded.

"Speak to me and tell me what we have done to offend you so." Yet no reply was heard or sensed.

From the corner of his eye, Weenuk caught movement from Wishna-hea. She quickly drew her knife from its sheath, and before she could plunge the blade into her stomach, he instinctively grabbed her wrist. Now everyone's attention focused on Wishna-hea.

"Why do you seek to do this thing, Woman?" Weenuk's thoughts said to Wishna-hea. In the upper world, words were never necessary. Thoughts alone were the standard form of communication.

"It was I who has angered Manitou. I must die."

Weenuk sensed her thoughts and replied, "Until we have the answers, no one will die. Surely there is enough death beneath us."

His hand gently lowered hers and took the knife from her. He looked deeply into her eyes, and his words echoed in her mind. "You are my woman, and you shall live long."

Silence covered them like blankets. No one spoke or even thought. They all closed their eyes and thought deeply. With Weenuk's lead, their thoughts were directed towards Manitou.

"Where have our people gone?" His thoughts projected out to them.

"Nearly all of our people will soon die." The voice of Manitou rang out. "And as they die, our ways will be forgotten, forever."

Total bewilderment swept over each of them.

"Why and how will our people die?" Weenuk asked.

"The white man will soon cover our lands and chase us away. Those who do not run will die. Like the blight that kills our trees, they bring disease to our lands."

Weenuk replied, "Then we shall make war against the intruders and chase them from our lands, like we did to the Iroquois."

"Their weapons are great, and they have no fear of our magic!" Manitou's voice echoed.

"Then we shall unite all our brothers and slay them all." Weenuk's voice became pronounced and his words snapped.

"Their numbers are many, and unlike those who live in the lands of the Iroquois, there is no end to their numbers. Their numbers are as vast as the stars in the sky." Manitou's voice remained unemotional.

"Then we shall attack them quickly, while their numbers are few and kill their sickness."

"We cannot win, and our people will perish."

"How can we stop this, Great One?" Weenuk questioned.

"I have chosen one to live among the white men. She shall not only live among them, but as one of them." He spoke decisively.

"How will we know this one?"

"You already do!"

Weenuk choked up inside and he blurted out, "Surely you can't ask my woman to do such things."

"I have spoken!" Manitou said sternly.

Before Weenuk could react, he heard Wishna-hea's voice, "I understand your wishes, Great One, and I shall do as I am commanded!"

Weenuk was shocked to learn that Wishna-hea could hear and speak to Manitou.

"Woman, why did you not tell me of your ability to speak to Him?" His thoughts turned quickly to Wishna-hea.

"She did not know, oh wise Weenuk, that I can hear her thoughts. Now I have allowed you to listen." His voice drifted away.

The smoke in the lodge faded and all were once again seated as they were before the journey had begun. No one spoke, instead they looked at each other in bewilderment. The only word that came to each of them was, "Why?"

None could address it. Not even Weenuk with his infinite wisdom, so it remained unanswered.

Finally the silence was broken.

"Do we tell the others?" Chief Amable du Fond questioned.

"It would serve no purpose. Our people would swarm to the Gorge and perish with the fishes. Without hope, no one can survive." Weenuk replied.

"We came seeking advice about Wishna-hea, and we are told that we will all perish. It must be her that has angered the Gods."

"It is not her that has sealed our fate, but that of time." Weenuk paused. "It is time for the white man to live among our trees, fish our rivers, and raise little ones."

"When will our destruction come?"

"When the winds of death cover our lands." Weenuk replied as he looked at the fearless Chief.

Silence once again prevailed.

"Is there nothing we can do to stop this?" The Chief asked.

"We must send someone to live among the whites and learn their ways, as well as teach them about our people and the wisdom of our ways."

"And who would this warrior be? Surely the strongest of our people." Chief du Fond quipped.

"No, it is I that must go!" Wishna-hea answered softly.

Silence once again blanketed the lodge.

"But you are a woman, and the woman of Weenuk. You must follow in his place. That is why he has chosen such a young woman."

"He has chosen me because it was Manitou's wish. It was His choice, not only Weenuk's. Now both have chosen me to live among the whites." Wishna-hea's soft voice became sharp.

Little was spoken of this outside the lodge. Each of the council members became morose and spoke only to each other. They feared word of their fate would accidentally slip out.

Weenuk told the village members that Wishna-hea would be banished from their lands and had to go live among the white man. Everyone had questions, but he needed more time to work them out.

# Chapter 6

Weenuk spent many hours in his lodge looking to Manitou for the answers to his questions. He heard about how the white man had treated the women of other villages, and would not allow that to happen to his woman. He would avenge such treatment with all his powers. But he knew that he must not interfere. He trusted the traders at the trading post even less, for they always cheated his people and would most likely trade her to anyone that had enough money to satisfy their greed. He didn't know how he could give his woman to a stranger, even less to one that he distrusted. He thought deeply on this.

Wishna-hea also shared in his worry. She didn't know how she could live among people she had learned to avoid. The only thing she knew for certain about them was that the men who cut trees often raped the women of her tribe, and she feared them. Certainly Weenuk wouldn't cast her into the arms of one of those vial creatures, would he? Would this mean that she wouldn't be able to come to the river she loved so much? Would she be allowed to see those she loved so deeply? Her mind swam with questions. She thought of nothing else and hoped that the answers would be found in time.

The others of the council dwelled on the grim future of their people. A cloud of gloom covered them like the darkest cloud. They hoped Weenuk, with all his power and wisdom, would come up with a solution. They had watched him closely when they were seeing the vision, and they knew of his private conversation with Manitou. Their attention had been divided between watching him and the spectacle beneath them. They all spent many hours in silence pleading with Manitou to give Weenuk the strength and wisdom that he needed to perhaps resolve their bleak future.

On the third day, Weenuk called the others to his lodge. Finally the answers came to him, and his confidence returned once again. When the elders began filing into his lodge, Weenuk and Wishna-hea were seated by the fire pit, hand in hand. Their heads were lowered, and a deep sadness hung heavily over the lodge. After the Chief entered, Weenuk finally lifted his eyes and nodded a gesture of welcome to the others. Normally, this would have been considered an insult to the others, but on this day, everyone understood. After everyone was seated around the fire pit, Weenuk began to speak without the normal formalities of an elder gathering.

"I know all of you share in my deep concerns about everything we have witnessed, for it is the future of all our people that must be decided. There are many things that must be discussed, but this is not the time for open discussion. Instead I will share with you what I have decided to do."

He looked deep into Wishna-hea's eyes before he continued, never breaking the contact with their tightly clasped hands. "My woman must leave our village forever! She must go live among the white men that encroach upon our lands and seal our future. The ways of our ancestors must be honored, but we must also understand the wisdom that Manitou gave us."

He continued without allowing time for comment from the others "Wishna-hea has been granted the ability to speak to Manitou directly. He has chosen this. It is through their discussions that I have been given the answers to my deepest concerns. You must all honor my decisions, and keep sacred all that I share with you for the wisdom comes directly from Manitou, Himself."

He waited for each of them to nod in agreement before he continued to share his decision with them. He discussed that in five days time Wishna-hea would be brought to the lodge of a horse trader named Tom. Of all the white men, Weenuk trusted him the most. He was always honest with the Montagnais, and appreciated the quality of the horses they brought to trade. He was without a woman and treated all people fairly. They would bring some of the horses that had been given as gifts from other villages and offer them as payment for her fair treatment. The trader was shrewd and knew horseflesh well, so they would bring only the finest horses.

The council agreed with the wisdom of his plan. Wishna-hea would have to be banished from her people and their lands. Weenuk would not allow his woman to be the seed of their death. No mention of the fate of their people could ever be spoken of— not to other village members or between themselves. Fate must take its time, and although known, must be ignored. It was best for the people of the Montagnais.

They would spend several days honoring Wishna-hea and paying tribute to the woman who would lead her people into their future by giving them hope. She had proven her love for the people of her village, as well as for Manitou.

The smudge pot was filled with the sacred herbs of tobacco, sage, sweet grass, and cedar. After Weenuk completed his ritualistic prayer and smudged himself, Wishna-hea rose and smudged each of the council members in the manner of the ancestors, which was followed by the lighting and smoking of the sacred pipe. At the completion of the ceremony, everyone sat in quiet meditation, each sharing their own individual thoughts with Manitou.

The smoke rose to the top of the lodge and out the smoke flap and eventually to His home. Secretly, Weenuk also prayed for his woman's safety and new wisdom. He prayed for the spirits of all their people. Weenuk then prayed privately that Wishna-hea's wisdom become even stronger than his. His heart was deeply saddened, and he dreaded a life without her. He could barely remember a time when she wasn't a part of his thoughts and hopes.

Wishna-hea was saddened by the realization that in the past few days, Weenuk had aged considerably before her very eyes. Today, he looked older than any member of their village.

The village began to bustle with excitement. There would be great festivities. Riders were sent to neighboring villages and announcements were made about Wishna-hea going to live with the white man. Members of the council were successful in spreading the word that Wishna-hea would become a missionary of the Montagnais. She would go to the white man and tell him about her God and people. She would also learn the ways of the white man and teach him about her brothers and sisters, so that all may live in harmony.

All, but the old, prepared to make the journey to the village of Wishna-hea. The mere mention of her name pumped excitement into the veins of and the neighboring tribes. The trails to the village of Weenuk and Wishna-hea became well traveled almost overnight.

The second day became a wave of unending well wishes. Some had traveled the entire night to be among the first to arrive. Shelters were erected and the best locations went quickly. Some of the villages brought their finest horse as an offering, in hopes that theirs would be selected to travel with Wishna-hea on her journey to the white man's world. The dancers brought their regalia and prepared to do their best dancing. This was an event that would never be equaled, so nothing was spared.

Weenuk's eyes rarely left Wishna-hea. She felt his eyes upon her and she kept her head lowered, while completing her woman's work. Neither of them had the courage to speak, so they remained silent. His hand often reached out to pass her something she required, but usually he just liked to hold her hand. Each time their hands touched, a wave of thoughts passed between them. They both had the power to talk with Manitou, so verbal communication became unnecessary. It seemed as the hours passed, they had less and less time together. There were so many guests, and everyone wanted to be in Wishna-hea's presence.

Wishna-hea blocked out her emotions and became the happy woman the others wanted to see. Weenuk became solemn and walked slowly to his lodge. He had enough of the visitors. He would see no others. Although pleased to host such an occasion, Chief Amable du Fond watched the pair closely with saddened eyes.

The Chief's power as a fearless and just leader had always been known, but in recent days, it had escalated to an even greater level. However, his thoughts on this day were not on his own status, but on the life of his lifelong friend. He watched Weenuk silently and shared in his grief. For many years he observed the connection the sachem had with Wishna-hea. He somehow felt that Weenuk knew from the beginning that this child would not only become his woman, but her greatness would far outlive either of them.

Only after Weenuk had time to himself did the Chief scratch at the entrance of his lodge. After he had been given permission to enter, the Chief motioned to three warriors that were passing and told them not to allow anyone else into Weenuk's lodge—that is not until Weenuk, himself, told them otherwise.

After Weenuk saw his friend's eyes, he reached into his bag and brought out his pipe. The two of them sat beside the fire pit in silence. When they finished smoking the pipe, they started a conversation.

"Weenuk, you knew back then, didn't you, that she was the one?" The Chief questioned.

"Yes, I did my friend. Now I must give her away!" Weenuk's words trailed off.

Their friendship had lasted a lifetime and it afforded them knowledge of each other's thoughts, so no other words were necessary. They sat in silence and watched the flickering flames and embers of the small fire.

Later that day, the Chief inspected all of the horses that were brought and made his selection. The three finest were to become the ones that Weenuk would offer the trader. The others would be offered as prizes for the games. The Chief's wisdom, once again was validated.

As darkness covered the village, the size of the fire increased. In fact, the flames of the central fire reached so high, the entire village was illuminated. The chanting began softly and soon picked up its pace. The drumbeats stirred everyone's emotions.

The dancers from the villages came out in their ceremonial regalia as the drummers began. Their costumes were as colorful as the spirits of the dancers themselves. For many of the dancers, it had taken years to complete their outfits. Each of them wore their regalia proudly and boldly, as the dancing began. The drumming continued as a murmur and eventually built up as the dancers spirits blended and became a symphony of sound and motion. They called out to their ancestors. The flames of the Sacred Fire reached upwards to the clouds, and became a beacon.

The dancers pronounced their strength, courage and skills as the drums pounded to the rhythm of Mother Earth. They danced to honor their love and compassion for Wishna-hea, the woman who held their future. They danced to give thanks to Manitou, for He had granted them this woman, and had once again pointed out the direction their people must take. But most of all, they danced for each other, because it was this union of brotherhood that allowed their people to survive for thousands of years.

Wishna-hea squeezed Weenuk's old and weathered hand. They looked into each other's eyes and their minds conversed. They planned to walk in the direction of the woods and quietly slip into their lodge.

A few days ago when all of the events started to unfold, Weenuk gave Wishna-hea a potion designed to rid her body of the unwanted growth. Now her body was seedless. The drum beat and the chanting blanketed all other sounds, so the sounds of ecstasy went unnoticed.

The lodge was without light and Weenuk could only hear the sound of his woman's dress being pulled over her head. His excitement grew as he envisioned her beauty. He untied the sash around his waist. In the darkness they sought each other. First, their hands touched and they drew each other in. His arms went around her waist and their lips met. They held each other tightly and felt their spirits blending even closer. No words or thoughts were exchanged. Their passion and love poured out to each other. As their spirits grew closer, the years seemed to fade away from Weenuk's old and weathered face. Each time Wishna-hea opened her eyes, the lines of wisdom disappeared before her very eyes.

That night sleep came to neither Wishna-hea nor Weenuk. Although their bodies were pressed together, they both stared off blankly into the darkness, as the dancing and chanting lasted well into the night. The others gained little sleep as well, although for different reasons.

Weenuk was the first to arise in the morning. He stood and raised his arms up in the air and stretched his body.

"Somehow you seem more spry today," Wishna-hea said to her man.

He turned to her and responded, "The spirit that I have planted shall not grow until He feels it is time. You must tell no one of this, for the evil ones will try to kill our son. He is the hope of all our people."

She reached her arms to him and he pulled her to her feet. Their arms wrapped around each other. There were so many questions yet unanswered.

After their talk, she walked briskly to the ditch and relieved herself, then she headed to the river to bathe.

"Oh River of Endless Beauty, of all things, I shall miss you most." Her eyes were peering deep in its spirit. "My powers have grown and I can hear the words of Manitou, yet I have never heard you speak my name or tell me of you. I have loved you more than any other. I have felt the strength you have nurtured me with. I have felt your pulse and smelled your breath, but I have never heard your voice." Her voice trailed off.

She would not allow herself to insult the spirit of the waters by not joining it now. She didn't dare toss her dress aside. There were people and lodges too close by, but then gave into her desires. "I must join you, one last time!"

She raised her arms up and looked warmly at the river. She pushed off with her legs and catapulted her body into the river.

The water rushed up to greet her. Her feet kicked and her arms moved smoothly, propelling her deeper. The water caressed her body as she swam on.

"Your beauty pleases me." The words filled her mind. She thought for a moment, then realized its source.

"You can speak to me!" Wishna-hea was elated. "Tell me more, and let me hear your voice."

She stopped her forward movement and looked around her as she turned in the water.

"You spin, unlike a fish, my friend. Is this your dance for me?"

She turned even faster, trying to see a face or image. The water of the river only sparkled.

"Don't you see my face, oh precious one?"

"Why do you call me these names? What have I done to earn this?"

"You have been His favored one, and I was sent to guard you. I am sorry, for I have failed you." The voice was deep and lonely.

"But how could you have failed me? How could that be so?" She said, puzzled.

"I should have stopped their horses, and swallowed them whole, but the Great One forbade me to interfere. There should have been something that I could have done."

"You have done nothing wrong. It was as He commanded. Nothing could have been done." Her warmth radiated and warmed its spirit.

"Thank you, my child, for you have given me back my respect, and oh, I do have something that I must share with you. It was I that had given you your name. Weenuk heard it from me! Goodbye, my precious one. I shall miss you."

Wishna-hea broke the surface and swam to shore. It took her a few moments to catch her breath. It had been some time since she had taken a breath. She felt drained, and yet refreshed. She sat for a moment and thought of the river's words. Now she understood their special bond.

As she dried herself with the softened deer hide and straightened her dress, she prayed, "Please, Great One, give me the strength to do this. My knees are trembling and my heart is broken. This is where I belong, but yet I know that I must leave all of this, forever. Do not let Weenuk see my weakness, for I know if he does, he will not permit me to leave regardless of the consequences."

She walked silently back to her lodge and closed the flap. She wanted no company. She reached down and grasped the hem of her damp dress and slowly peeled it over her head. She looked down at her stomach and pressed her palms against it.

"I know not when you shall see the world, but I shall protect you forever." She thought to the dormant spirit that was harbored within her. Then she slid the dress that the women of the village had prepared for her over her head and looked down to examine it closely.

She then placed the sage in the smudge pot and smudged herself completely. She knelt silently, saying good-bye to everything she knew and loved. Unable to connect with her spirit, she remained silently grieving. She wanted to join her spirit and once again laugh and play, but knew it was gone, and soon another would be sent to her. Never again would she smile, for the essence of her spirit that she had known all her life would soon leave her.

The morning of departure came too soon. Wishna-hea held all of her most cherished possessions close to her chest, while tears streamed down her cheeks. Her life was ending, and there was no way of preventing it. She was not allowed to take anything, except her clothing. The doll she played with as a child was the most difficult to part with. She cradled it against her breast and rocked it as if it were a live child. A lump formed in her throat. The tears streaked down her face and trailed down her dress. She could not control her sobbing.

She laid the doll upon her bedroll and slid it between the hides. She kissed her fingertips and placed the kiss upon the doll's head. "Farewell my friend. You shall be with me forever in my heart."

She stood and faced the entrance. Her feet would not allow her to leave. She looked around the lodge and engrained every single item into her mind so it would be there forever. She reached down and picked up her medicine bag, which contained the remains of Weenuk's finger and clutched it to her breasts. This was the one thing she could never part with. She thought of hiding it among her clothes, but instead hung it proudly, once again from her neck. That pride allowed her to lift up her head and walk boldly through the entrance.

The flap opened to the morning's sun and it welcomed her with pride. The Earth, the sun, and the spirits knew of her greatness. The birds sang out louder than anyone ever remembered. Both the Eagle and the Hawk circled high above. She stood just outside her lodge and took a deep breath. The only evidence of her sadness was the tear streaks down the front of her dress.

A procession of riders awaited her. Weenuk was seated in the front of the procession. His left hand held the reins of his most prized horse. Upon its back was the blanket the women of the village had made for her.

When Wishna-hea saw the horse so personally blanketed, she almost lost her composure. She looked into Weenuk's eyes and heard his thought. "I am proud of you, my woman. Now make them all proud!"

She gained strength through his thoughts, and she acknowledged it with a smile.

"Will you take me now to my new home and people?" Her voice was loud and crisp, though her heart was trembling.

She grabbed the horse's mane in her left hand and slid effortlessly onto its back. When she was seated a whoop echoed. Each of the party raised their hands and shouted loudly to their ancestors.

# Chapter 7

The procession was comprised of many braves on horseback, as well as the women from their village and surrounding villages. Those of prominence rode proudly on horses, and the women of lesser prominence were on foot. Because of this, the ride became a journey. What started out as a small escort now became a large procession.

They wound their way through the massive white pines, along the bank of the Amable du Fond River, crossing the narrow passage at Eau Claire Gorge. The tracks that were once blood covered were now pounded deep into the Earth. The river was proud to be with her, one last time.

No one spoke. In fact, the only sounds that were heard were those of the unshod horses and the nearly soundless footsteps quietly passing on the hardened Earth. Weenuk's eyes often darted away when Wishna-hea looked to him for conversation. No longer did she dwell on worry, because now it had been replaced by excitement. Her world had come to her to bid her farewell. The reality of it finally settled in, and she accepted her bid in life. These were her people, and she was ready to make these sacrifices for them.

She turned on her horse and gazed at the spectacle behind her. Obviously, everyone else shared in her excitement. Their eyes and smiles matched their enthusiasm. Her eyes were wide and her heart beat proudly. She turned back and looked at her man. He looked into her eyes and his mind said, "No greater honor could any warrior achieve. Our people love you, and would gladly die at your feet, so you may live. Yet you allow your love for them to take you away." His thoughts paused. "Your love for your people and their love for you, have dwarfed the heaviness in my heart."

They passed the rest of the journey in silence.

Off in the distance they heard the sound of a bell and the excited sounds of men. The men at the sawmill scrambled for their weapons. Some had rifles, others pistols and yet others only brandished axes. They numbered only twelve men, but they were ready and willing to inflict as much damage on the Indians as possible. They would not go down without a fight.

Eugene Varin was the foreman. Many said that he was the first lumberman to cut down a tree in these parts. He gripped his rifle tightly. His huge arms filled the red flannel shirt as he huddled behind the logs that were stacked close to the carriage.

"Which of you buggers have been messing with their women again?" He hollered out, not really expecting an answer. "You're gonna get us killed this time!"

Charlie and Tom Smith had a shanty down by the mouth of the Amable du Fond River, and each had a rifle peering over the logs.

At first, the loggers only saw the first handful of Indians, but now the procession grew longer and longer. The men hunkered down and each prepared for death in his own way. If this was how their maker had meant for them to die, then so be it. They were going to give it their all.

"Look, they have their women with them!" someone shouted.

"What the hell do you suppose those redskins are up to?" Eugene questioned anyone with a possible answer. "What the hell are they doing with their women?" He repeated to himself. "Somebody get me the looking glasses," he hollered out sharply. He snatched the field glasses from the man's hand.

"Let's go take us a look-see and see what the hell is going on. Let's just hope them buggers are as peace loving as the preacher men say!" He watched the procession still growing, as he scurried to a better vantage point.

His eyes focused through the tubes and looked intently. Back and forth he scanned the seemingly endless line of Indians. Women were mingled, and many were on foot as the procession continued on. This totally baffled him. They dragged no teepees and it was too early for their summer migration. There were no children either. The glasses made the distance much shorter, and he was torn between anxiety and amazement. "Some of them aren't even carrying weapons. What can you make of that?" He mumbled to himself.

Charlie raised his voice sharply, "Don't think they're looking for no trouble!" After a moment he continued, "Hell they even got a woman leading the bunch, and an old man. Do you think this might be some kind a religious thing or something?"

The dozen men watched anxiously as the Indians rode by with little regard for the white men. Eugene continued to scan the line back and forth, searching for a clue. Finding none, he searched closer.

"Well, I don't think we're gonna have a shooting match, but we sure as hell aren't having them for tea either!"

Some of the warriors in the procession were beginning to become anxious, riding in full view of the loggers with their rifles trained on them. Their horses sensed it, and this caused a small ripple effect through the procession.

Weenuk and Wishna-hea sensed the tension building and paid no attention. They would be passing the mill soon, and all would become calm. Their horses' paces remained constant. They eventually turned west, away from the mill.

The sun had long ago crested and was halfway to the trees before they came to wooden lodges with the flat tops and square sides. There were three buildings that formed a semi circle around a building that had smoke coming from a stack of rocks piled on top of the flat roof. There were endless lines of fencing that were made of strong branches and trees that were locked together.

There were no signs of life other than a bucket of water that had recently been spilled on the ground. Weenuk smiled to himself. The signs of haste pleased him. Before the sun got much lower, he would build on that fear. The horses in the round corral paced nervously and milled around.

Weenuk raised his right hand and signaled the procession to a halt. Chief du Fond kicked his horse's side and rode up to join with the two.

"Perhaps we should have sent a rider to warn him and tell him of our wishes," the Chief stated to Weenuk.

"He has no reason to fear us. Come and we shall tell him of this." Weenuk replied as he kicked his horse's side gently. He turned his horse to face the procession and spoke loudly,

"We shall speak to the trader and tell him of our plans. Do not bring the horses up until I signal, and you shall guard my woman." Weenuk ordered those who had ridden closest to him and his woman. "Wishna-hea, you remain until the time is right, then I shall signal for you."

He jerked the reins and spun his horse around, heading for the cabin. The Chief's horse quickly joined him, along with four of their bravest warriors.

Three riders came up along side of Wishna-hea. Their chests pushed out proudly, and their heads held up high, as they watched the six riders approach the cabin. The necks of the six horses were arched and their hooves stepped proudly.

The barrel of a rifle poked through a notch in the timbers and a voice shouted out, "What do you want from me? I paid you fair for your last horses!" His voice crackled from fear.

"We come in peace and bring gifts!" Weenuk's voice carried. He raised his hand and signaled the riders. He spoke in the language of the trader. This he had learned from the Nipissing that lived near the trading post. After a signal by the Chief, three riders came forward, each holding the reins of a magnificent horse. The horses' heads held up proudly and their long tails waved. The riders led the horses past the Chief and Weenuk. They rode past the front of the cabin and displayed the beauty of the mounts.

The cabin door opened slowly as Tom stepped out. His rifle held in ready, but his eyes sparkled at the magnificence of the horses. His eyes scanned the lines of the horses. Rarely had he ever seen, let alone owned, such beauty. He lowered the barrel of his rifle, looked at it, then looked up at the massive number of redskins that were only a short distance from him.

"Don't think you'd do me any good, just piss them off," he chuckled to himself and leaned the rifle against the cabin and took two steps forward. "What are you looking for?" he shouted out.

The Chief and Weenuk both nudged their horse's sides and rode forward. Their escorts followed a few paces behind, ready to strike with deadly force if need be.

"I am Weenuk, the spiritual leader of my people and this is Chief Amable du Fond. We come in peace. We bring gift of horses." His words came out loud and clear, though somewhat mixed between the two languages.

Wishna-hea sat anxiously upon her horse. Her legs spread wide to accommodate the horses muscular back. She strained her ears to hear his words, but could hear nothing but the footsteps of the fidgeting horses. They talked long, and her nerves peaked. She tried hard to listen to her man's thoughts, but he had blocked them off, so that she could not hear them.

The entire procession hugged the tree line. Each member was anxious to learn of the developments, and silently leaned forward on their horses. Each of them was trying to hear a single word or glimpse a single gesture.

They watched as the trader first stood nervously, then took steps towards the horses. He stopped abruptly, and then catching himself, looked to the seated riders for permission before proceeding. When he was granted permission, he first stroked the flank of the closest horse then ran his hands down the horse's leg and to his foreleg. He lifted the horse's hoof gently. His examination was thorough. His hand traveled back to the horse's back, while he spoke softly in a monotone whisper. He sought out even the slightest imperfection, and found none.

"This is gonna cost me a fortune." Tom thought to himself. He then went to the second horse, and followed the same procedure. Then he went to the final horse. He finished the last inspection much slower. His mind was racing.

Without thinking, he put his hands on both hips and stood square to the rider. The warriors snapped their bows up abruptly! The arrowheads pulled back to only inches from the wood. Their arrows were aimed directly at his heart.

Tom's heart skipped a beat, and snapped into his throat. Urine trickled down his leg. He froze in his tracks and couldn't move a muscle, as perspiration covered his brow.

"Do not move!" Chief du Fond's words shot like a bullet.

"Oh God, what did I do?" Tom's mind went blank.

Wishna-hea's heart leaped! "No!" Her mind snapped.

Immediately, Weenuk felt her word's impact, but paid it no heed. His hand flipped up from the elbow, signaling to hold. "Speak!" He commanded.

Only "Help!" squeaked out of Tom's lips. Tom swallowed hard. "I meant no offense!"

"Then lower your hands and we shall speak further!"

Weenuk's bargaining power just increased.

Everyone's horses settled down and many of the riders dismounted to stretch their legs. Conversations became relaxed. Wishna-hea sat motionless, watching her man and the others. Time passed very slowly.

Finally, one of the escorts rode back towards Wishna-hea, in a dead run. The ground whisked past the horses hooves and within minutes he pulled on his reins and the horse stopped abruptly. The warrior looked proudly at Wishna-hea. His eyes sparkling he beamed with pride. "Weenuk wishes you to come with me!" Her moment of truth had finally arrived.

Together they rode back at a leisurely lope. Wishna-hea's eyes were opened wide, taking in everything she possibly could. Her heart beat rapidly, as a bead of sweat trickled down her spine.

She viewed the corral, large and strong. The cabin was longer than wide. There was a single door and no other openings, except for notches in the logs, which his rifle had pointed out from earlier.

The structure that housed the horses was far larger than the cabin, but her eyes now focused on the trader.

She had expected a much older man, and was surprised to see that he was young. A full beard covered most of his face, and he was a large man. Not fat, but powerfully built. She watched his eyes riveted on her as she approached. She could tell he had stopped talking abruptly when he saw her, for her man gestured for him to finish speaking.

She directed her horse to stand next to Weenuk's, while looking deeply into his eyes. "Does he wish to have me?" Her thought was projected to Weenuk.

"He has agreed to keep you for one year, perhaps longer." Weenuk informed her, but added, "From watching his eyes when you approached, I believe he will keep you longer!"

She had no idea what they spoke of before she arrived, and perhaps would never know, but at least she would be safe. From the urine marks on the front of his pants, she knew they had frightened him seriously, and she knew he would not dare treat her badly. Again looking into his eyes, she saw kindness. She continued scrutinizing him further.

Weenuk spoke to him, but his eyes could not be pried away from her. Apparently he had expected a much less attractive woman. His eyes followed the contours of her body, from her radiant face to the moccasins on her feet. He viewed her differently than he did the horses, but with equal intensity.

A few more words were spoken, then Weenuk and Amable du Fond kicked their horses' sides and rode back to the others. Their escorts rode closely by their sides. Wishna-hea turned on her horse and watched them ride off. The entire column of riders were whooping and hollering with their hands raised high in the air.

When the leaders rejoined the column, they rode past the lead, and with the single raising of Weenuk's hand, everyone knew the meeting had gone well. Their woman would be treated well. They would still have to ride past the lumbermen with their rifles, but the tensions would be less.

Wishna-hea sat upon her horse and watched as the last riders left her view. She remained there long after they had disappeared, uncertain what to do. Tom stood with his arms hanging at his sides as he watched her intensely. Her beauty overwhelmed him. He drank in the beauty of her face. Slowly his eyes wandered lower as he closely examined the way her dress was pressed to her body, and his smile broadened.

He finally broke the spell and said, "Come!"

Though not knowing the word, she knew its meaning, and she slid from the horse's back. She led her horse and one of the others to the corral. He took the other two, leading the way. She patiently waited until his horses had run off before she walked in to release hers. She clutched both her blanket from her horse and the bedroll with her clothing rolled neatly inside.

He was standing outside the corral gazing at his new possessions. The horse she rode dwarfed the beauty of the others, though their beauty far surpassed any he had seen. He watched as she stood there looking in the direction of the horses, but he knew she was not watching them.

"What do they call you?"

His words sounded garbled and totally impossible to understand. She watched as he tapped himself on the chest and said, "Me, Tom." The sounds were similar to what meant the droppings of a snake, but she doubted he meant that. Still she chuckled to herself.

She reached down and cupped her hands in the horse's watering troth. Then, slowly brought the water to her mouth, for her mouth felt drier than the sands of the riverbank.

"No, No!" Tom shouted as he raced towards her. Startled, she jumped back. Calmly and gently he took her wrist in his hand and led her to the pump where he began pumping on the handle. The water surged from its spout and poured on the well cover.

Her eyes lit up in amazement. No one had told her that the white man had magic, too. She brushed his hand from the pump handle and began to pump it herself. She smiled broadly as the water continued pouring from the pump. She pumped again and again, the water splashing all over the front of her, and she laughed as she pumped more. The tension had been broken.

Tom's eyes sparkled and he quickly put a bucket under the nozzle. He looked at her and nodded his head, with a twinkle in his eyes.

She understood him perfectly, and her fears dissipated quickly.

He gently took her by the wrist and signaled her to follow him around the entire property. He showed her the horses that were in the corral and the building where he kept the grain and the hay. Her eyes were amazed at the intricacies of the large stack of trees that were woven together. He showed her where the outhouse was, and she didn't understand until she looked inside the round hole and caught a whiff of the air inside. He brought her inside the cabin where tack and saddles lined the entire walls. Short sections of tree limbs, which had been fastened to the logs with metal loops and iron nails, provided good support for the large saddles. She had no knowledge of what the large pieces of leather were for, but could smell the horses on the leather, and surmised the uses.

He then showed her the wooden frame that was raised on short logs, which made his bed. A thick bed of moss covered the bottom, and she pressed her hands into its softness. There were also scratchy blankets that were rolled in a heap. A pair of pants hung from a short branch that was jammed between the logs.

The floor was dirt that looked as if it had been pounded hard with a flat stone. She continued looking around the cabin. There was no light, except for the light that filtered through the slots in the walls and doorway. Strange stones were hanging from the walls and one was on the wooden surface that was raised from the ground. The stones could be seen through, and there was a liquid in the bottom. She held up the one that was on the table and shook it.

Tom laughed and took it carefully from her hand and set it back upon the table. He reached into his shirt pocket and pulled out a wooden match and scratched it against the back of his legs and it ignited.

Wishna-hea jumped back and her eyes became huge. She dropped her blankets and flipped her knife from her waistband, instinctively.

She startled him as much as he had her. His eyes were even larger than hers. When seeing his reaction she wearily laughed at him and stared at the burning match that was very close to his fingertips. A small squeak escaped from his mouth and he tossed the match into the air, and then quickly stuck his fingers into his mouth.

She chuckled nervously at him, lowered her knife and then put it back into its sheath. He realized how silly he looked and he began to smile coyly. She did not know of his words but she read his eyes perfectly well. He liked her.

She enjoyed the next few days and weeks. Most of her fears diminished, and she watched him intently. She did not understand the reason for the fire burning inside a metal box. As best as he could, Tom used sign language to explain its purpose. She quickly understood, but could not remotely understand why one would cook over it, especially at this time of year.

Tom stayed busy out behind the horse barns, and when she came near him, he chased her away. She shrugged her shoulders, then wandered the grounds, inspecting all of the buildings. The barn that housed the horses was made of logs that were buried deep in the ground and there were spaces between each of them. They formed a large circle, measuring perhaps thirty of her footsteps. The roof was made of large logs laying close together, hollowed out. She examined this closely. The logs were placed with the split and hollowed side facing up, and a second course of logs lay on the top of them. They, too, were hollowed, but they fit snugly on top of the others. The hollowed sections were locked together. The front of the building was higher than the back, so that the heavy snows and rains would run off to the back of the buildings. The rectangular roof hung over the sides for more than double a man's height. This, she assumed, would shelter the horses and keep their droppings from the inside of the building's floor.

The four horses that came with her wandered the corral by themselves. There were large fields that lay behind the corral, where several other horses grazed. A small creek wound its way through the fields. The grass was just beginning to turn green, and she looked out at the animals and knew. Manitou had prepared this day, long ago. He had provided for her, well.

Weenuk spent many hours each day in deep mediation with the spirits of the Upper World. He sought the wisdom and conversations of Manitou. He asked many times what the eyes of the Eagle saw, and if his woman smiled. When he lay on his bedroll at night and stared into the darkness, his thoughts were answered quickly. Her voice filled his mind, and questions were exchanged. During the day he would feel her presence frequently, and knew their spirits were still as one.

Inside the cabin there were piled iron pots and pans and bags of corn. There was a pile of grain for the horses that spread out wide. The contents of the room nearly filled it and provided only enough room to allow passage to the bed and to the small table. When she slept at night the only place large enough for her bedroll was by the table, and even that had to be moved.

Tom busied himself with making a bed for Wishna-hea. The bed was made of strong birch posts, and for the base of the bed he carefully split beach to make a flat base. When finished making the bed frame, he laid it flat upon the ground. There would be no point of putting legs on it, for he knew she preferred the ground. They could be added later. He then cut the thick bed of moss to fit the frame. This would be much softer than the ground, and when he had time to get to the trading post, perhaps he would pick up a mattress. He stood back and admired his handiwork. Her bed was actually made better than his.

Weenuk told him that she was to learn the ways of the white man, and he thought this would be a good beginning. He lifted it above his head and walked to the door of the cabin.

Wishna-hea was at the pump, filling a bucket when she saw him carrying the bed over his head and heading for the door. She leaned against the well and put the bucket down, crossing her arms in front of her. She watched as he carried the bed to the door and leaned it up against the wall, while opening the door. His head did a double take, and he put his hand on his hips and laughed. Guess there was some rearranging to do.

It didn't take much imagination for her to realize the dilemma he was in. She chased him away from the cabin and gestured for him to go and tend to the horses. After putting up a resistance for a bit, he turned and walked to the corral.

Tom began introducing the new horses to the herd gradually. He opened the paddock and allowed the new horses to go up to the edges of the other horses' pasture. The other horses moved to the common boundary in mass. One horse stepped from the others and walked boldly up to the newcomers. The leader of the four stepped forward. Both of their ears were pointed forward then laid back on their necks. The leader of the large herd stamped proudly with his right hoof, and snorted towards the ground. Cautiously, Wishna-hea's horse raised her head proudly with her eyes focused intently, and squealed. She held her ground. The language of dominance between all animals is fundamental. Despite her superior breeding, she nuzzled against the lead horse's neck and whinnied in submission. There would be another day to challenge authority.

Tom watched this with great interest. Their adaptability to new herd was one of the key factors in the price of horses. Some fought viciously and caused injuries. After some snorts and a couple of nips, the new horses settled in.

After watching the integration, Tom turned and walked back to the cabin. "Oh my God!" His jaw dropped. Nearly every single item in the cabin was now out in front and Wishna-hea was heading back in for another load.

"Ho, hold on there!" he shouted as he picked up his heals and ran slowly to the cabin. She made her point without words.

On one side of the cabin, there was another building, which housed his smithing tools. The roof was high enough to accommodate a large draft horse, and nearly half as wide as the cabin. There was a fire pit built out of stones that was high enough to allow Tom to work on the shoes without having to bend over. A large anvil was about four feet from the pit. A bellow was permanently attached to the pit. The bellows could quickly intensify the flames and easily soften the metal of the shoes. A wooden tub of water was placed close to the pit for quenching and tempering the metal. Boxes of various sized shoes cluttered the side of the doorway and long pieces of iron lay against the wall. These Tom could use to make his hardware or even shoes, if need be. A full keg of shoeing nails was open and the various hammers, tongs, nippers and rasps completed the building's contents.

Tom stood in front of the building, and began writing on a piece of paper. He paced from one side of the building to the other and wrote down a number. He did that with the depth of the building, as well. Tomorrow he would send word that he was willing to trade a horse for some lumber from one of the mills. There were three in the area, and he wanted to have all three notified. All of them would be eager to accommodate him, but he had to see who was hungrier for a new horse. He would be prepared to spare two horses, if the quality wasn't too high for either, but he was a shrewd horse trader.

# Chapter 8

Wishna-hea stretched out in her new bed. Her eyes focused on the total blackness of the cabin. The moss felt good as she lay on her back and looked upwards. When her eyelids were closed, she saw bright and clear. When they were open, she saw only darkness. She closed her eyes again and blocked everything out. Her world became filled with an illuminating haze. She had the sensation of floating and began to spiral upward. She passed the waterfalls of Manitou's home, and though standing erect, she continued floating to his campfire, which burned brightly. She sat upon her heals, as was custom for a woman beside the fire, and waited for His appearance.

Time had no meaning, so it went unnoticed. The aroma of sweet grass filled the air, and there was a warm and gentle breeze. Although the night was pitch black, she saw all things clearly. A strong feeling of power surged through her, and she felt its beauty. The clarity of her thoughts amazed her, and she sat and absorbed her surroundings. She felt a presence, though her eyes saw nothing. The feeling became gradually more intense, and the aroma of sweet grass became powerful.

Out of the smoke from the fire, the image of a man materialized. He was old, and the wrinkles of his flesh were many. His nose was prominent and his eyes were brilliant. There was intensity in them that she had never seen before in any man, not even Weenuk. His jaw was clenched. He sat upon a shimmering blanket with his legs crossed. He was dressed with a deerskin loincloth and soft moccasins. His shoulders were broad, and his chest still muscled, though showing deterioration from age. His skin was old and weathered. His lips curled downward.

"My child, the road you have chosen will not be an easy one. You will learn of the white man's greed and lust. Some may treat you badly, for you are not one of them, but you will also find the truth in hearts that love you. You will see goodness in all men, for that is your nature. You hold, within your body, the spirit of a son. Right now, it sleeps like the great bear in the season of snow. It shall sleep until you wish it otherwise. Your son will look as you wish, but be cautioned. As he looks, so shall he become. Teach him wisely the ways of our people for he holds our future."

His body transformed itself back into the smoke, and rolled leisurely up to the stars.

She sat totally still. Her mind beckoned him back, for she had many questions, but he would not return.

"What did he mean? How would I know how to do these things, and could I do them correctly?" She was troubled, her eyes became heavy and she drifted off to sleep.

Her eyes snapped open and she clutched the blanket to her chest. She sat up abruptly and looked around the room. The sun was beginning to rise and light filtered through the small ports in the logs and the sides of the door. She sat there, looking over the entire room, searching for something, but she had no idea what. The dream of last night was so vivid and real. She felt like the smoke from the fire had clouded her mind, and she had to sit and clear it.

When she cleaned the cabin out, she had rearranged everything. Her bed was now only three feet from his, to allow both to walk between them. She would have preferred to sleep in the center of the room, but she arranged the headboards against the wall.

She looked at Tom and he was sound asleep. His bed was raised above her bed, and she could just see his side. He slept upon his back, and his right hand hung over the side. She rose to her feet, slipped into her moccasins, and walked out the door. The morning sunlight shimmered across the dew-covered grasses.

The horses were grazing close to the barn, and the sound of a rooster broke the stillness of the dawn. She was growing accustomed to the noisy bird's awakening call. Today she enjoyed seeing him fly to the top of the fence post and announce a new day to the world.

Tom would be waking up soon, so she skipped to the well, drew a bucket of water, and placed it upon the well. She slid her dress over her head and bathed. When she was finished she joyfully dumped the bucket upon her head. She shivered with delight and shook the water from her skin. She smelled the dress and decided she would go to the creek today and wash her dress, as well as Tom's shirt and pants. He put on his change of clothes yesterday.

She picked up a bunch of kindling and placed it in the small fire pit. There were still embers burning from the day before. She knelt down and blew the embers softly, and a small flame erupted. Some small branches caught quickly and within minutes the fire burned brightly. She swung the heavy iron pot over the flame and began reheating the soup. She had taken two potatoes from the cabin when she came out, and now she sliced them thickly and threw them into the soup. Then she added some more water and a small amount of herbs. There was still meat in there from yesterday, so they would have a fine morning meal.

At first, Tom had been a bit apprehensive to sample her cooking, but he soon discovered that her cooking far surpassed his. Since he would be waking up soon, she felt it her duty to have his meal ready.

She had been practicing his name, "Metom . . . Metom . . . . Metom." She said it over and over to herself. This was the morning she picked to say his name. She looked down at her dress and brushed her hands over the material to brush away the fuzz from the blanket.

"Maybe I should wait until tomorrow after I have washed my dress?" She thought to herself. Then she dismissed it.

When he woke up, he opened the cabin door and headed for the outhouse. After he finished and washed up, he came back into the cabin and saw Wishna-hea sitting at the table with two bowls of soup. He nodded to her, sat down and picked up his spoon. He was ready to dig into the bowl, when Wishna-hea grabbed his wrist and said, "Metom."

He looked at her blankly, and then his eyes lit up. His smile showed his handsome white teeth. He brought his palm to his chest quickly and said, "Me, Tom. Not, Metom."

She looked at him puzzled, shrugged her shoulders and touched her lips with both hands. "Metom," she repeated.

Tom put his hands on his hips and thought for a moment. "Let's see here, girl. How are we gonna do this?"

He sat up straight and dropped his shoulders and faced her squarely. He held his right hand up in front of his shoulder and said, "Me." Then he swiftly sliced his hand through the air, in front of his mouth. He continued by patting himself on the chest saying, "Tom."

Wishna-hea's eyes lit up. "Tom," she said distinctly and patted him on the chest. Her eyes sparkled and she repeated, "Tom" over and over again.

Tom beamed with pride, and he looked at her with a puzzled look on his face. He raised his finger and pointed at her.

Wishna-hea patted her chest and said, "Wishna-hea." She patted her chest again and repeated it. Seeing there was no sparkle in his eyes she repeated it again.

Still, the light remained out. He didn't have a clue. She slowed down her words, and still not even a flicker. "W-i-s-h-n-a-h-e-a."

"What's in hey?" He scratched his head and tried again.

"Wish my hay?" He said, still puzzled. "Why don't I just call you Nellie? Yup, you're Nellie." He patted her on the chest twice and said, "Nellie."

She took his hand in hers and said, "Nellie?"

She held his hand pressed against her chest, and his eyes were glued on the placement of his hand. Beneath his hands was her breast, and he was uncertain if he should pull it away. This had no meaning to her, because breasts were considered for infants and children to suckle and play with. She did, however, see the look in his eyes, and understood. She held his hand in hers and moved it over the swell of her breast, and she watched his eyes grow. She felt an unusual power over him, and it stimulated her. His hand remained on her breast and he began to squeeze. He felt the warm firmness through the buckskin dress. His trousers were becoming tight. Her eyes caught a glimpse of the movements and knew her power over him was increasing rapidly. She gently removed his hand from her breast, and she took a step back, and in one quick movement pulled her dress over her head.

He stood there looking at her naked beauty. Her breasts were firm and the nipples were dark. Her skin was smooth and flawless. Her hips were shapely. He stood there with his eyes wide open gazing at her nakedness. It had been more years than he cared to remember since he last saw a naked woman, and she far exceeded his expectations of beauty. The stirring in his loins was finished, and his trousers were totally cramped.

Nellie stood in front of him, amazed at the impact her body had on him. Her jet-black hair still wet from the morning's bathing, hung nearly to the base of her spine. She stood motionless before him.

He stood motionless in front of her. His eyes moved over her entire body. His mouth opened and his hands hung loosely at his sides.

She reached out and took his hand in hers, and placed it back on her breast, and his other hand came up quickly and took the other breast in it. He squeezed them both roughly. He continued squeezing both breasts and finally reached down and sucked the right one into his mouth. He began sucking hard on it. His left hand dug deeply into the other breast's flesh.

She had not yet bore a child, so the sucking on her nipple caught her totally off guard. The stimulation immediately went to her loins and she desired more. She took the back of his head and pulled him away, moving his mouth to her other breast. The other women never told her of this feeling. She enjoyed it greatly.

Weenuk sat close to the fire pit in his lodge. His eyes were closed and the smoke curled up, drifting through the smoke flap.

His palms were turned up and resting on his thighs. His face pointed upward and he remained in deep meditation. He focused his thoughts on the floating flame that lead him deeper and deeper into the world of his ancestors. He would not see anyone, for to see them, he must sit and smoke tobacco. They would come after he had lit the pipe to welcome him. Today, he wished not to sit with them but to share thoughts with Manitou.

He sat before His fire pit. The host had not arrived yet and he sat patiently. Shortly afterwards, he took out the pipe and by using two small sticks, he picked up a burning ember. Then, he placed it into the bowl of his pipe, drew the smoke deep into his lungs then held it in. Time has no meaning in such places, so he waited for the feeling then slowly exhaled. The smoke passed over the flames of the campfire. His smoke mixed with the smoke from the fire. The smoke intensified then began to swirl. The flames quickly flared up with intensity then subsided. Manitou once again sat directly across from him, with his arms crossed.

"Your heart is heavy, Old Friend, but your woman is safe. The trader has given her a white man's name and as we speak, she is becoming his woman."

Weenuk felt unsure of his heart. He sat in silence and looked directly at Manitou.

"But my heart is heavy. I have watched her every day since she was a child."

"I have spoken to her and told her that she carries, within her, our spirit."

"I am troubled Manitou. I no longer have the power to speak to her at night, and tell her of our village and her friends."

"Nor does the river or the tree. For now she lives in a world that knows no such things." The words echoed through Weenuk's mind.

"How can I know of her, if I am no longer able to speak with her through my thoughts?" He questioned.

"She knows of your heart, and that shall never change. She is a strong and good woman, and will endure whatever she must. She knows of her duties, and shall carry them out. For she knows that she is the hope of our people."

Weenuk sat and stared into the darkness. His old friend sat before him and the two exchanged more thoughts.

"Many in the village wish to ride and speak with her, and learn of her new life." Weenuk's thoughts were heavy.

"You must keep them from her, for she needs time to adjust to the ways of the white man."

"But it is I that wish to see her." His voice tapered off, and his eyes lowered.

"I know your heart is heavy, but our people's needs must surpass yours. If you wish, choose another to warm your belly and prepare your meals. That is permissible."

"But I wish no other, Great One, for we share our spirits." Weenuk's thoughts lingered on.

The smoke once again swirled and then rose, as smoke does. Weenuk sat long and mourned the absence of his woman.


The morning passed quite quickly and the noontime meal needed to be made. Tom was riding to the trading post. He needed more supplies. He also wanted to let the owners of the mills know that he needed to trade horses for lumber. The thought of taking Nellie with him crossed his mind, but he thought better of it. He would just let news of her slip out in idle conversation, to test the waters.

Nellie picked up his pants and shirt from the floor, and turned towards the door. Tom's eyes watched her and focused on her rounded backside. Just as she walked through the door, his mind kicked in and he leapt to his feet, running after her.

He stood in the doorway naked, holding a wash board in his hand. "Nellie, you will need this!" he shouted while holding the board high in his hand.

Hearing his holler, she turned around and noticed him holding something in his hand. "What is that strange thing?" she thought to herself.

He went to the side of the building and took the large tub he used to bathe in and put the washboard inside, dragging them both to the pump. He then went back to the barn, brought out a trough that he had made from two boards, and leaned it in front of the pump into the tub. He then pumped the handle, and she figured out what he was doing.

"They have such strange things, but this one is good." She thought to herself.

Shortly afterwards, he made his intentions clear to her. She was to remain at the cabin, while he hooked up the team and rode to the Hudson Bay Trading Post. The ride in would take just about two hours if he took his time. That would give him adequate time to figure out how he would let things slip to the busy bodies at the post.

It was a real pleasant ride. The day had turned out warm and sunny. The trail to the post was well traveled. There was a fork in the trail that lead to the sawmill. The ruts in the trail were deep from the many wagons that had traveled it. There were several places where the trail crossed small creeks and even a few that were not so small. In heavy rains the trail was all but impassable with a wagon because the river's waters became perilous.

It had not rained in well over two weeks, so the rivers and creeks were calm, and passage was easy. Tom pulled out his sack of tobacco and rolled himself a cigarette. He usually didn't indulge in tobacco, but on the long ride to the post, he enjoyed a smoke. The image of Nellie's beauty passed his mind several times on the way, and more than once his pants became snug.

He pulled his team up to the hitching post in front of the trading post. There were several lumberjacks who rode in with two wagons. He had barely lowered himself to the ground when one of them came up and began talking to him rather excitedly.

"Damn! What the hell did you do to get them redskins all riled up? Hell, even the damned old man hasn't seen that many Indians at one time in his entire lifetime!" he exclaimed.

"So much for the practiced speeches," Tom thought to himself. He forgot that the procession had to pass the mill.

He only laughed at the question, but by the time he reached the door to the post, three of the other men came up and had more questions on the same subject. By the time he was actually inside the post, two additional men walked up to him with great big smiles and loads of questions.

Tom had never been the center of attraction, but he enjoyed it. He puffed out his chest and raised his hands. "Listen up!" he spoke loudly, "Seems like Old Weenuk had a big problem he needed me to help him out with." His face beamed with pride. "You know, he knows I have all this good horse sense and all. He needed my help bad, too," he continued.

"What do you mean, Tom? What sense do you have that those red fellers don't have?" One of them asked.

"You see, they have this notion that they want their folks to learn about us, so they have this Indian living with me and I'm teaching them how the white man's world works!" Tom blurted out with pride.

"You mean, you're gonna teach the Indian how to bugger his buddies when they come to trade horses?" Another commented humorously, which brought about a loud round of laughter.

"What are they really doing Tom? Teaching you how to take care of there horses?"

"Maybe I can use one of their young ones to do my chores." Another added. "But do you have to feed them, too?"

"Nope, she feeds me good." The words slipped from his mouth.

"She?" the agent blurted out. "You mean, they have one of those big Indian squaws keeping you buggered up?"

The whole place roared with laughter. "It seems we have a squaw man for a horse trader now. How many horses did you have to give them for the old squaw?"

"Well, it didn't cost me a damned thing, as a matter of fact. They gave me some fine horses, and she's damned pretty, too."

"Now, we have a situation here. We have a horse trader trying to horseshit another trader. Sounds like a whole lot of shit to me!"

"And she has these damned pretty teats, too." Tom added.

Everyone roared.

When Tom told them that he wanted the mills to trade him

lumber, the place broke out in chaos. It seemed he wasn't lying, after all.

It took nearly an hour to get the supplies he needed packed in the wagon. Most of that time had been spent passing comments back and forth with the men. It had been a long time since he had laughed that hard, but it was now time to head back home and finish tending to his chores.

He gave the horses a bit of the whip and they picked up their pace. It would feel good to have a hot cooked meal when he got home. And just maybe, he could have some more of the other stuff tonight, too.

# Chapter 9

Nellie stood watching him trim the hooves of the horse. His tools were different, but the results were the same. Then he clamped firmly onto a metal shoe for the horse and stuck it into the embers of the fire and began working the bellows. Nellie had seen the tracks of the white man's horses many times before, but never saw why they were so different. She watched with keen interest.

The shoe quickly became red hot. He then pulled the shoe from the forge, fitting it over the rounded end of the anvil. Then by pounding with a large hammer, he began reshaping it. A second heating was required to complete the reshaping. While the shoe was still hot he pressed it solidly into the hoof of the horse to complete the perfect formation. Some nails were tapped in, nipped, and then tapped flatly against the hoof.

This amazed Nellie. When he finished, she lifted up each hoof and inspected closely. The shoes fit like a piece of wet rawhide. She was beginning to understand and enjoy the wisdom of the white man's ways.

She seemed to have a way with horses. At first, only the horses from her village would come to her when she entered the pasture and called them. Then slowly each of the other horses became familiar with her presence. After accepting her, she then began to encourage them to come to her. She accomplished this by shaking a bucket of grain. When this didn't work, she would toss a small handful of grain on the ground. It was a slow process, but eventually most of the horses came to her.

A great deal of her spare time was spent with the horses. She found it easier to communicate with the horses than with the man that was keeping her. Unlike Tom, rather than spending her time working with them, her time was spent mostly playing with them. She knew the importance of having the horses accept and trust her. She even taught her horse to play tag. She slapped its flank, and then raced across the pasture. The horse playfully chased her and took its time running up behind her. It then gently tapped her on the head with its chin, turned and ran across the pasture while she chased after it. The game continued until she no longer had the strength to run. She simply dropped down onto the ground and sat, waiting until the horse returned to her.

Life with the white man was much more pleasant than that of her people. Her workload was lightened considerably. She simply cooked the meals, cleaned the cabin and washed the clothes once a week. Her life was filled with activities of her own choosing.

She spent countless hours brushing the horses, moving from horse to horse, constantly talking to them. Tom frequently watched her with the horses. At first, it was for her safety, then it gradually became an enjoyable activity for him. The enjoyment she gained from brushing them, he also gained. The beauty of her jet-black hair glistening in the sunshine outshone the beauty of any horse he had ever seen.

When men came to talk to Tom about horses, Nellie waited for him to tell her which horse they were interested in, then she walked out into the pasture, and quickly returned with the horse. A simple pat of affection on the horse's neck was all the animal needed to understand that it was to follow. Since she had moved in with him, he found that his profits had increased remarkably.

More than three weeks passed before Gene Varin from the sawmill showed up. The loggers told him all about Tom's business, and being a shrewd trader himself, he didn't want to appear too anxious about the trade or the woman that was now living with Tom. No matter how he tried to think it through, he could not figure out why an Indian would give his woman to a white man, especially a young and pretty one like Nellie. Since he first came here, he really didn't have any curiosity about the Indians' ways, but this situation intrigued him.

He was heading to the trading post after he left Tom's, so he decided to take the big wagon. He hitched a team that he had traded from Tom some years back, figuring that it would be good to show Tom how well he treated his horses. Being somewhat of a quiet man, he decided to take along one of the men who didn't talk much with him. It would be nice to have someone along to help him load the wagon up, but he really didn't want to spend the entire trip in needless conversation. He had a bunch of thinking to do, and no time for small talk.

He bellowed to his traveling companion, "Get up here now, and don't go trying to bend my ear either. Because I'm in no mood! And another thing, when we get to the horse trader's place, you stay put in the wagon! You got that? Now that we have that settled, maybe we can have some peace and quiet!"

He had a lot of questions he wanted to ask Tom about the Indians, and didn't want to start with any rumors that came from the loggers. He wanted to hear everything Tom knew about the Indians, and he couldn't wait to hear Tom's animated stories.

It didn't take long to get to Tom's place. He pulled up in front of the cabin and tied the team to the hitching post. "Stay put, you hear?" He barked to his riding companion as he got out of the wagon. By the time he turned around, Tom was waving at him as he and Nellie were walking in from the pasture.

"Heard you been looking for some lumber!" Gene shouted out when Tom was within hearing distance.

Tom waved, acknowledging Gene's anxiousness to do business.

Gene watched Nellie closely as they got closer. "Hmm," he thought to himself.

As they walked closer, Tom felt a twinge of pride when he saw the smile on Gene's face.

"So, what are you planning to build?" Gene asked as Tom and Nellie approached, extending his right hand. Their handshakes were firm as they quickly sized each other up.

"Good to see you, Gene. It's been more than a year, hasn't it?" Tom asked.

"Pretty near," Gene responded.

"You're looking fit." Tom said as he took a step back. "Must be the good life, I been hearing about. Want some soup? Nellie, here, makes about the best soup I've ever eaten."

"She's a damned fine looking woman, Tom, but why did so many of them bring her to you?" Gene was a man of few words, and if he had something to say, you knew it right away. Tom always appreciated his candor.

"I haven't figured that one out either. We don't talk that much, and I figure that may be a bonus, too." Tom laughed and quickly changed the subject.

"Do you think your rider wants some soup, too?" Tom held both his hands up in front of his mouth and made a sipping gesture, Nellie quickly went to the cabin and came back with the pot of soup she had planned on having for the noon day meal. Within a few minutes a flame was licking at the bottom of the pot.

"If I get them all fattened up, he won't be worth a damn when we get to the trading post." Gene spit out, while chuckling.

They passed pleasantries back and fourth while the soup was heating. Tom walked over and checked over his old team and smiled.

"The horses look good. It looks like you've been working them real good." Tom commented as he slapped one of the animal's on its shoulder.

"So, how have things been down at the mill? I heard you have lots more jacks coming, and they're bringing their families, too. Is that right?"

"That's kind of what I hear, but I'm not sure." Gene remarked, neither confirming nor denying. He didn't want Tom thinking that his horses were worth more than they were. More men would need more horses and the prices would escalate quickly.

Nellie handed them both bowls of steaming hot soup, and without a word or gesture headed straight for the barn. Using the spokes of the wheel for support, she climbed up to the seat and made her way up to the top of the hay wagon with the pitchfork firmly in her hands. When she reached her destination atop the wagon, she began pitching hay into the loft with fluid motions. Both Tom and Gene watched leisurely as they sipped on their soup. Neither man said a word until they were both finished. Then Gene complimented Nellie's soup.

Tom reached into his shirt pocket and took out a list of lumber that he needed. With a friendly gesture he handed the list to Gene. "This is pretty much what I figure I'll be needing."

"What are you planning to build?" Gene asked in a business-like tone. His eyes scanned the list quickly. Then he looked it over once again more closely.

"I'm putting up another shed, I guess." Tom replied flatly. "Well, it won't be much of a building, so I can't give you much of a horse. Let's go see what I can help you with."

They walked towards the fence. Nellie's eyes locked onto them intensely. The two of them climbed up on the fence and began pointing to different horses among the herd. Nellie continued watching.

Tom pointed, and Gene shook his head no. Gene pointed, and Tom shook his head no. The game of point and nod was a work of art. Both were skillful at their task. As the pointing and nodding continued, the tension between the men started to grow. After a short time, their voices rose and Gene's hands snapped upward, gesturing as if praying for supreme intervention. Tom spun around and snatched his hat from his head and crumpled it up in a ball.

The drama eventually ended with a civil handshake. The deal was done. Tom would be getting his lumber within a couple of week's time, and both were pleased with their bargains.

Word of Tom's horses was beginning to spread, and several men from the lumber camps rode out to see his horses for themselves. However, other men simply came out to get a glance at his Indian woman. At first Tom took their comments in fun, but then he started to become irritated by them. If the comments became too crude, he would make a simple gesture to Nellie and she headed to the barn or cabin. As soon as she was out of sight, the subject of the conversation was quickly changed, and business once again prevailed.

Nellie often felt their eyes burning through her flesh, and it always made her feel uncomfortable. Even though she didn't understand their words, she did understand their lustful looks and spirits, and because of this, she kept her knife hidden beneath her dress.

Finally the day came for the lumber delivery. A fine pairs of Tom's old horses pulled both of the wagons. After checking over the lumber, Tom compared it to his list. He then leisurely checked over both teams of horses. He sure has owned some damn good stock, and he traded them fairly.

The two drivers and Tom quickly began to unload the wagons. Nellie soon joined in, and in no time at all, the lumber was unloaded and separated into stacks. The new addition would be the first building on the property that would be made primarily of boards and not logs.

Nellie cooked and served the midday meal of cornmeal bread and soup. For the loggers, a change from their usual biscuit and bean meals was always a treat. The soup was made with fresh raccoon, potatoes and carrots. Fresh bark from the young sprouts of the black birch tree and a handful of selected leaves added greatly to the flavor.

The three men talked almost nonstop throughout the meal. Several times Nellie felt their conversations were about her, but she enjoyed listening to the sounds. The conversation seemed friendly and filled with pleasant laughter.

She was beginning to like the white men who came to see the horses, but not all of them. When buyers were interested in looking at horses, Tom always walked them to exactly the same place on the fence. When the game of point and nod finished, Tom pointed out the horse to Nellie and she retrieved the horse for him. When she entered the pasture, she often spoke soft sweet words to the horses, announcing her arrival. As she approached the herd, she maintained the same soothing words. The horses all knew her scent and trusted her. They simply followed her wherever she led.

Nellie was extremely anxious to see how a building was constructed. The wagons had barely left their sight when she took Tom's hand and lead him to the side of the cabin. It didn't take long before Tom understood Nellie's gestures.

"So much for not being able to get me working!" Tom thought humorously.

"Well, woman, looks like I'm not gonna get much rest until this damned thing is up," he said to her. Her understanding was increasing every day.

He went into the shed, took out a small sledge hammer and pounded in stakes for the addition's outline. It would be nearly twelve feet wide and as long as the cabin was now. He went back into the shed and brought out two shovels. One was brand new, and the other one he handed to Nellie.

Nellie was delighted. She took the shovel and held it out from her while she felt its heft, then she turned it around. She was totally excited about using a white man's tool for the first time.

Figuring it would be nice to have a root cellar, Tom and Nellie dug out a section of ground deep enough to allow them to nearly stand up in. When the floor was fairly even, Tom dug deeper at the corners and took out large rocks. He filled in the holes with flat stones and put in the corner posts. From ground level to the height of the floor he took forearm length sections of trees and stacked them up pointing outward. Then he packed them in with mud. This was designed to keep out the cold and give the floors better support.

Nellie proved to be a willing and able helper, and the construction lasted for several weeks. Between the chores and working on the addition, there was little time for much else. Tom was becoming more and more used to Nellie's questions and their language barrier was rapidly diminishing.

Word was spreading about the virgin forests and the loggers were becoming more and more plentiful. This meant more business for both Tom and the Hudson Bay Trading Post. Men always needed horses, as well as supplies. Rumor had it that some of the loggers were sending for their families, too. Prosperity was slowly filtering into the area.

A pow-wow between the area chiefs including Amable du Fond, Antoine Kikwiwisens, Beaucage, and Restoule was set to discuss the future of their people. Weenuk passed their words to Manitou, seeking His wisdom. Their escorts were many, and the bush was peppered with scouts. A solid ring of braves circled Weenuk's lodge and stood far enough away to avoid ease-dropping.

Inside the lodge, the fire pit burned brightly and the smell of sweet grass filled the air. The rhythmic beating of the drum called out to the Great Spirit, as the pipe of friendship was passed among them. The pungent aroma of tobacco mingled well with the grassy sweetness. The fire was burning and soon large stones were added to absorb the heat. Cold water was splashed on the stones and hot steam hissed, filling the air. As the sweat poured from everyone's pores, their thoughts intensified. No words were spoken nor thoughts conveyed. They sat in silence, seeking the spirits of their ancestors. Soon the Spirits came forth and stood in the smoke-filled lodge. The Great Spirit looked down upon them and declared them pure and worthy to sit in council.

The main topic was of Wishna-hea and her treatment. The eyes of the Eagle had watched over her closely, and had given Manitou a full report. Weenuk's wisdom was once again confirmed. His selection of white men was wise.

The acceptance of Wishna-hea in the white man's heart and life brought approval from everyone. It was apparent that the horse trader not only appreciated her company, but he also treated her with a level of respect that pleased all. She had quickly become accepted in the white man's world.

They spoke of the settlers coming into their lands. They were different than the ones who cut trees. They came only seeking a home and to live in peace. Both the men and their women were strong, and their children were eager.

A discussion soon ensued that they must show the white man an act of faith. After much debate it was decided that they would erect a wooden totem of their faith. Manitou was pleased with this, but he insisted that their gift must be greater. He wanted the elders to learn more about the white man's world.

The council meeting lasted long and many disagreed strongly, but in the end, it was decided that the wishes of Manitou would prevail. As much as some disagreed, His wishes must be obeyed.

# Chapter 10

The warmth of summer was approaching and the black flies finally retreated. The fields were lush and the horses shed their winter coats and began to shine. The planting moon was upon them and Nellie had to get the soil ready. She woke long before dawn and prayed to Hahwenniyu.

"Now is the season of growing things. Now we give thanks to our Creator . . ."

Her words trailed off and she began to sob. How quickly she had forgotten the simplest prayer. She bowed her head in shame. Since she came to live in the home of the white man she had not once said her prayers. Tears welled up inside her and she held them back.

"This was not the way of my people," she said to herself.

She breathed in a deep breath and held it. Then she gasped to exhale.

"What's happening to me? Why can't I hold my breath?" she thought to herself.

Had Manitou forsaken her? She had forgotten Him, and now did He abandon her? She gasped for breath and her hand grasped her breasts. She must try to make amends.

She moved quickly to the fire and added more kindling. Quickly the flames arose. She sat upon her haunches and began to hear the inner chant. The sound came from deep within her spirit and she chanted loud. She tossed a bundle of sweet grass into the fire, and the sweet aroma filled the air. The smoke began to rise and it circled her body. A great wind rushed against her as she was transported to His home. She raised her right arm above her head and proudly the Snow Owl alighted on her arm.

She brought her arm down and kissed the proud bird on its beak.

"I have missed you," she said affectionately to the owl.

"But I have not missed you, my little child. For I watch you each night, until the sun arises. Then I fly away and sleep and await the darkness so I can watch over you some more."

"I have missed you so, and I miss my Eagle. I wish to come home to you and my people."

"My child, I have taken you from your home," the owl said mournfully. "You can no longer walk back into the past. Only the future lies ahead. You are the hope of our people. If you leave the white man's home all of our people will die, and we will cease to exist." The words were no longer the owl's, but the words of Manitou.

"I long for my man and my friends," she thought, and then continued. Her voice became braver. "The white men do such dumb things, and act so strangely. They trip over their feet when my skirt gets raised in their presence. And sometimes, they get so excitable, they can't even speak."

Her voice became soft and mellow. "And sometimes, he uses my breasts to suckle, and sleeps with them pressed to his head throughout the night. Only a child does this, am I right?"

"How does this feel to you, my child?" The strong voice asked.

"It feels so strange and makes me tingle. When he is inside me I become overwhelmed. A feeling washes over me like the waves of Clear Waters."

"I watch him put iron on the hooves of the horses. He does it so well, and the horses love him." Her words trickled out.

"I see the stars in your eyes my child, and as you speak of the horses' love, you also speak of your own. It is true the horses love him, as they do you. But just as the horses love you both, you both love each other."

"No! This cannot be, for I love Weenuk, and only he!" She yelled out.

"It is true. Your heart is pure and filled with love for Weenuk. He was your man, and has loved you in return. But there is a difference Wishna-hea. You are in love with the horseman, and that is the best kind."

She thought for a moment, letting the words sink in. "Is that why I soak the robe each night, and why it feels so different and so magical?"

"That is the beauty of falling in love. Speak no more of this! I have no time for such foolishness." Manitou's voice bellowed.

Wishna-hea watched his eyes sparkle, and saw through his facade. Manitou had a soft spot, and she discovered it. He was a lover of love.

She became solemn and asked, "Have I offended you that deeply, Manitou, that you take away my very breath? I have done as you have asked and I am living in the white man's world. I have learned some of their ways and can speak their tongue. Why have you chosen to make me gasp for breath?" Her voice reflected her increasing anger.

"It is not me that takes away your breath, my child, for I am the giver of life. Your breath has become labored, for the source of your power has been shunned, and feels his presence no longer. Weenuk has observed this and has spoken of it to me. There is nothing I can do. Your powers are waning, and soon you will be as any other. This does sadden me, for also you will no longer be allowed to come to my lands and sit at my fire with me. This is the way things must be."

The fire became dense and swirled around her and she left the lands of the great Manitou for the last time.

The flames from the fire flared up as Tom watched from the doorway. He had watched her kneeling at her fire pit with her head hung down. He swore that he could see the flames of the fire through her body when he began watching, and he dared not disturb her. He stood at the doorway in total amazement as her spirit once again returned and made her whole. Then he turned and went back inside the cabin and never said a word about what he had witnessed.

The morning sun rose and looked down upon her as she knelt beside the fire pit. Its flames were gone and only the burning embers remained. Nellie stood up and stared into the embers. She felt a deep sense of loss, but her time for regret was over. She was no longer of her people. Even Manitou had abandoned her.

Nellie ran to the barn, grabbed her shovel and ran to the back of the barn. In a rage, she gripped the neck of her dress, and in one quick movement, pulled it over her head. Tears streamed from her eyes as she tried frantically to rip her dress, but the buckskin dress refused to yield. Regardless of how hard she tried, it would not tear. Throwing the dress to the ground, she then grabbed the shovel and began digging furiously. The hole deepened quickly. She grabbed the dress, and with all her anger, threw the dress into the hole. She then fell to her knees and began covering it with both her hands. When she finished, she pounded the ground with both of her fists. Her tears nearly turned the Earth to mud.

After she finished filling and pounding the hole, she looked up to the sky from her knees and sobbed mercifully, "Oh Manitou, I beg for your forgiveness. I cast away the clothing of my ancestors, for I have insulted you. You have given me so much and I have failed to honor you. I am not worthy of being one of my people that you have given so much to."

Slowly she rose up and walked away from the cabin with the shovel in her hands. When she was a fair distance away, she began plunging the shovel into the soil. Again and again the shovel dug deeply into the ground. As neatly as if she were weaving a blanket, her furrows took on a precisely even set of rows. Her pouch swung freely between her naked breasts in a rhythmic dance. She may have shed the dress that covered her, but she would never part with the final token of her man's love.

When Tom swung the door open on his ritualistic trip to the outhouse, he caught a glimpse of her in the corner of his eye.

Snapping his head up and staring at her, he said to himself, "What the hell is she doing?"

"Nellie . . . Nellie what are you doing? Where is your dress?" he shouted at her.

When she refused to answer, he started to walk, then run towards her, pulling the shirt off his back. As he approached her, he realized that she was crying.

"What's wrong? Where is your dress?" he blurted out as he grabbed her and wrapped his shirt around her. He then wrapped his arms around her and held her tightly.

The tears flooded from her eyes and her sobs belched out. Her knees seemed to give out and he lifted her into his arms and carried her back to the cabin. It was some time before her sobs stopped and she was able to explain as best as she could her failure to her people. Tom held and rocked her in his arms as he gained a clearer understanding.

"It's okay, Nellie. I will buy you a new dress, and do anything I can to help you." He placed both hands on her cheeks and lifted her face to him. Tenderly he kissed her lips and she knew he not only understood, but he shared in her grief, as well.

With that understanding, she wiped away her tears. She wrapped her arms around his neck tightly and kissed him warmly on the lips. His shirt seemed to radiate security to her, and she now understood his love for her and her love for him.

She stood up, held her hand out to him and said, "You stay."

She turned and walked out, heading back to where she began digging earlier. Tom rushed out, took her by the hand and said, "Come, I'm gonna show you how we do that."

He walked into the barn, holding her by the hand. "This is a plow," he said in an instructional tone. Then he walked her over to the harness that hung on its pegs. "This is the harness for it, and I will show you how we hook it up. Come on."

He draped the harness over his shoulders and with a quick movement, he pulled the plow away from the corner and began dragging it outside of the barn. When she made a gesture to help him, he held his hand out and said, "No, you are gonna need all the energy you have. You just take that harness out and I will show you which horse to fetch."

She understood him completely.

When he was finished hooking the horse and plow together, he began his instructions on how to use the plow. She caught on quickly, and soon her tears were all but forgotten. She beamed with pride as she hitched the horse and began plowing her first garden.

At first she was more intent on looking at how the plow worked than where the horse was going. But after a few shouts from Tom, she quickly learned how to make her furrows straight as if she was using a shovel.

With this new knowledge, she quickly understood Manitou's wisdom. He was trying to show her that the white man's way could benefit her people and more pointedly, the women of her people.

Tom stood back with his arms crossed and a satisfied look on his face. The more he looked at her, the stronger his desires became. Before he knew it, his desires became too strong, so he walked out to her, took her by the shoulders and kissed her hard on the lips. Soon her shirt and his pants were thrown on the ground and they were locked in a lover's embrace.

She broke off their embrace as soon as he was satisfied, and she put his shirt back on. Immediately, she headed back to plowing the fields.

After pulling on his pants and finishing his morning ritual in the outhouse, he decided to head down to the trading post to pick up some supplies. While he readied the horses, his head swirled with worrisome thoughts, "What if some of those loggers come around to look at horses? Those dirty bastards aren't gonna turn the other way, that's for damn sure!"

He went into the cabin, took his gun off the pegs and headed to the field. When he reached Nellie, he handed the gun to her and told her to shoot any man that came near her.

At first she didn't quite understand, but after he put the gun to his shoulder and squeezed off a shot into the woods, she understood his meaning. She didn't have a clue about how to use it, but she agreed anyhow. He looked at her with uncertainty and then convinced himself that it would be safe leaving her alone. There hadn't been any new folks in the area for a while, and he figured she would be alright. He wouldn't be gone that long anyway.

Weenuk looked down upon her and a tear trickled down his old, weathered cheeks. Although he was not allowed to speak to her, he watched incessantly from above. Manitou had failed to tell the whole truth. Weenuk not only loved his woman, but he had loved her since she was a child. She was a special woman, and she had taken his heart many years ago. Perhaps that explained why, up until the night before she left his lodge, he had never violated her purity. He loved her as a child and that love would never change.

When she became his woman, he was the happiest man in the world. He loved the warmth they shared, and was always content to just touch her hair or feel her flesh. Though his face was old and weathered, his heart was young. She took away the sorrows and turned his world to joy. He wished she could have lived with him forever, but that was not what must be.

She jumped up and down and whistled, just as Tom had showed her. Her sense of accomplishment filled her entire being. She could have plowed the entire field. She hummed to herself while the horses pulled along, then she hollered, "Ho!" and "Back!" so she could get the horses to move in the right directions. Up until that day, she only knew that horses could pull a wagon full of supplies. Now she had a new respect, and also a new game for the horses.

The sun was high in the sky as she plowed on and on. She stopped and waited impatiently as the horses rested and drank water. "Hurry you old nags. The crops will be ready to harvest before I finish my work!"

Out of the corner of her eye she caught movement and

snapped her head around. First she saw the faces of the horses passing the barn then she saw the team with Tom inside.

In an instant, her heart leaped, then dropped. She had gotten so involved in plowing that she had totally neglected to prepare a meal for him. She lifted the blades of the plow from the ground and tried walking, but the plow was too heavy. Before she knew it Tom was at her side ready to offer assistance.

Tom looked around and shook his head. She had plowed up more than double the size of his usual garden. She and the horses looked like they could use a good rest. After he unhooked the horses and lead them back to the barn, he handed her two packages.

Even before she took the packages from his hands, she wrapped her arms around his neck, kissed him full on the lips, and made growling sounds. He stood with his arms at his sides, holding a package in each hand, while her arms were wrapped tightly around his neck. Her eyes sparkled, and her kisses were passionate. He couldn't speak, because her lips were pressed too hard for him to be able to do anything but enjoy. Finally, he dropped the packages, wrapped his arms around her and returned the kisses with equal passion.

After a while, Tom broke free from her embrace and picked up the two packages on the ground. He handed them to her with a proud and smiling face. She reached out, touched the packages and said, "What?"

The packages felt stiff in her fingers, and when she squeezed them, they made a crackling sound. With a puzzled look on her face, she squeezed each package again.

It finally dawned on him what the problem was. She had no idea what a package was, or what she was supposed to do with it. He gently tore a small piece of paper from the package, revealing a hint of its contents.

After catching on, she tore the package open and lifted her arms into the air. It was the dress of a white woman! It was the color of a clear sky and had buttons going down the front. The buttons shined and were the color of the snow. She held it up in front of her, and her eyes filled with excitement.

She slipped the dress over her head and looked down at herself. She put on a big smile. In fact, it was the biggest smile Tom had ever seen on her face. She looked at the buttons as they twinkled at her. They were shiny like the pebbles in the river. She studied them briefly then tucked her first button into the buttonhole. Her smile broadened even further. One after another, she worked the buttons. There were five in all.

With a pleased look on her face she turned to the fire pit and started warming their soup. Tom could not have been more pleased with her reaction. While she was occupied making their meal, he walked back to the wagon and returned with one of the wooden boxes filled with supplies. A few minutes later he walked out of the cabin carrying a frying pan and a mixing bowl. He walked to the hen house and came out with two eggs in his hand. Then he called Nellie to join him.

As she stood watching him, he reached inside a tin can and took out two handfuls of a powder. Then he opened a small tin and shook a little into the bowl. Next he cracked open two eggs and dropped them into the bowl with the powder.

Nellie watched him in fascination. She never saw a man with a bowl in his hands to mix anything. What he was mixing, she had no idea, but he was mixing something with a total look of satisfaction on his face.

He stood up and came back with a bucket of water then he splashed a little into the bowl and began mixing it together. He added a little more water then walked over to the fire and put the pan on two rocks. When the pan was hot, he smeared a piece of salted pork on the pan and made it sizzle, and then he poured the batter into the center of the pan.

Nellie was wide eyed, and she sat upon her haunches watching him. "Was he now going to cook?" she questioned herself.

While the food was cooking he ran quickly into the cabin and came out with plates and a jug of something. The mixture formed a circle and began bubbling over the heat of the fire. With the flip of his wrist the contents made a perfect somersault and landed face down in the pan. A short time later he slid the flat substance onto a plate, took the jug and poured a small puddle off to the side of the plate. Then he rolled the flat cake up and dunked it in the syrup. He brought the dish up to her mouth and allowed her to taste his cooking. She had never tasted anything as sweet or good. She marveled at the flavor, and quickly took another bite. She would remember this day, always. It was truly a day of firsts.

The rooster had barely finished its call, when she woke up and slid her new dress over her head. The other package was placed in the center of the table and remained unopened.

She excitedly shook Tom's shoulder and woke him from a sound sleep. He slowly sat up, yawned and stretched in the most peculiar way. "It isn't even light out yet? Come back to bed and snuggle up. We can get up later. There's nothing special to do today anyhow."

She took his hand and nearly pulled him from the bed. "Come!" she said, as she continued pulling him by his hand. "Come" she repeated.

While he was sliding into his pants and lacing up his boots, she was out at the fire pit rekindling the fire. By the time he got outside, she had the fire blazing and she stood there holding both the bowl and frying pan out to him.

He walked off of the porch and out to her. Still sleepy eyed, he mumbled under his breath, "I knew I would live to regret that."

He took the bowl and frying pan in his hands and laid them on the stones by the fire. Then he got up and walked back into the cabin. Within two minutes he came out with a metal pot with a glass ball on the top.

"Well, if I'm gonna teach you how to cook, I sure as hell am gonna teach you to make coffee."

He filled the pot with water, dropped in a handful of coffee grounds, put the cover back on, and put the pot on the cooking rock. He made the pancakes, showing her slowly how much of each ingredient he put in. He knew that she would have a problem flipping the pan, so he brought out a spatula and showed her how to use it. By the time the third pancake was done, the coffee was ready and he poured it through a tea strainer.

She quickly spit out her first mouthful. Tom almost fell over backwards laughing so hard. She didn't think her reaction was funny at all, but after seeing his reaction, she decided to take another taste. Her next sips were much smaller. She had tasted many of Weenuk's medicines, but never one that had such a pungent taste. She paused and thought for a moment, then reached for the jug of syrup and poured a little into her cup. She took another sip slowly and swirled it around in her mouth. Pleased with her solution, she smiled and took another big swallow.

Tom's eyes opened wide and he looked at her. "Didn't take you long to figure that one out, now did it?"

As soon as the morning meal was finished, Nellie went into the cabin, slipped her new dress over her head and put his shirt back on. She did not want to wear her pretty new dress when she had work to do. While Tom was in the outhouse, she fetched the team of horses and placed the harness on the ground next to the horses. This time she watched eagerly as Tom put the harness on the team and hitched them to the plow. By the time the noonday sun reached its peak, the ground was tilled and she stood gazing at Tom with a look of total satisfaction on her face.

Tom drove the team back to the barn, unhooked the plow and then hooked them up to what he called, the "honey wagon."

When the horses were ready, he drove the wagon to the back of the building and, with Nellie's help, filled the wagon with horse manure. Then he pulled the wagon to the garden and together, he and Nellie, shoveled the contents onto the soil. She understood giving back to Mother Earth, but this activity was new to her.

They filled and emptied three more wagon loads of horse

manure into the garden. Then Tom hooked the horses back to the plow and tilled the soil once again.

She watched the moon at night and waited for the moon to smile at her with its full round face before she would do the planting. It was six nights before the moon became full and Manitou had given His blessings.

The garden was planted with seeds of corn, beans and squash—the foods of her people. Tom also showed her how to plant potatoes, beets, carrots and peas.

When the planting was completed, she went to the barn where Tom was shoeing another horse. She took him by the hand and lead him back out to the garden, where she said her morning prayer, asking Manitou and Mother Earth for their blessings for a good harvest.

Tom was beginning to understand her ways. He was also becoming aware that her people's belief in their Great Spirit was perhaps even stronger than the beliefs of the preacher men who tried to teach him religion.

He heard from some of the loggers that a man named Father Bruel was giving religious teachings to the Indians, and he wondered if they should be teaching the good preacher instead. He watched Nellie throughout the day and counted the number of times she prayed to the Great Spirit, and the number far exceeded any man he had ever known, including the preachers.

Back in the cities, people heard rumors that the lands in the northwest were so fertile that the simple dropping of a seed assured a bountiful harvest. The trees were so big a man could spend nearly an entire day just cutting one down. The ribbons of rivers and lakes intertwined in such a vast array that a logger could choose which river to take. A logger could make a fortune. Even though the lands were totally uncharted, the Indians were mostly friendly, and one could live in safety. It was reported that game was so plentiful that people did not have to go more than a few paces from their homes to end up with more than they could eat in a year. The rivers were teeming with fish that were larger than a child. There was even talk that the government was going to be opening up the land for anyone who had the backbone to work it.

In the beginning of May with temperatures rising well above freezing, the sun began melting the deep snows. The threat of heavy snow had diminished and the passage was finally considered safe. The trip from Gravenhurst would be a little better than a week's ride. The foreman of the men who were in charge of setting up the mills and camps began his long journey. The wagons were laden with supplies and men. The ground was still frozen and passage was easy. It would take eight days, if all went well, to reach the timber area. There would be plenty of time for the other loggers to get there before the spring run off.

That night as the blankets were tossed from the bed, a seed of a different kind was fertilized.

*"And my massive wings spread wide as I rushed to tell Manitou of the planting."*

# Chapter 11

The settlers began their migration. Each week the numbers rose. Their canoes floated in the water, laden with supplies and dreams. Their backs and hearts were strong, their faces proud, and their eyes filled with wonder. The majestic beauty of the land surpassed their wildest dreams. The fish were bigger than the stories and the bush was teeming with life. The vastness of the land inspired them. They wanted to make this land their home.

Chief Amable du Fond and Weenuk listened to the reports of the many canoes of white man filtering in. They knew the truth and wisdom of the vision they shared with the others . . . and the old men got older.

After seeking counsel with Manitou, Chief Amable du Fond divided his people and set out for Allumette Island on the Ottawa River. This enabled him to watch over and control the main route to his lands. Each year the white man migrated to the island during the months of warm sun.

The island was a day's ride, but with the women, children, and supplies, it would take two. Fishing was good and the berries and wild rice were plentiful. Life during the warm months was easy, and dispositions always improved.

Tom began to show Nellie how to cook different foods including baked beans, biscuits and fried eggs. He showed her the way to prepare his eggs the way he liked it. She showed him how to make corn meal, fish and wild rice. And she showed him how to cook her meat the way she liked it.

Their days were filled with new experiences. Within months she began to understand Tom's language. Although he was picking up a few of her words here and there, she was learning his language and the thoughts that encompassed them.

One day he walked into the cabin to find her holding one of his books. The book was open and she exclaimed, "You teach!" She excitedly began her reading lessons that day.

When Nellie asked Tom to take her to the trading post, he reluctantly declined. He knew that the only women who went there were the whores who took the loggers and traders money. However, he also knew that there were Indians living in teepees near the trading post.

By this time, everyone within a hundred miles knew Tom had an Indian woman living with him. However, she wasn't like the ones who lived near the trading post. She was different. She was his woman and he liked that, and he didn't want her to change one bit.

One sunny afternoon, Nellie heard the hooves of running horses pounding on the dirt road towards their cabin. She hollered excitedly to Tom who was in shoeing a horse. The sound of the horses' hooves grew louder. Tom instinctively reached in the cabin and grabbed his gun.

He could see a cloud of dust on the road and hear the thundering hooves. The whoops of Indians were muffled by the sounds of the many horses. Nellie reached up under her dress and pulled out her razor sharp knife, and held it point down. The sounds of Indians grew louder. Tom cocked a shell into the chamber and raised it close to his shoulder.

Nellie stood next to Tom on the porch. The shouts of the braves echoed against the trees. Immediately after they came into view, she spotted her two older brothers. With a jubilant whoop Nellie leapt into the air waving her arms above her head.

As soon as Tom realized her excitement, he scurried to the gate, pulled the logs back and opened the paddock. There were fourteen horses in all. Most of them were young and spirited, but others were wise and trained.

Nellie's oldest brother charged up to the porch and snatched her up in his arms, still managing to stay well seated upon his strong and powerful horse. Her arms wrapped securely around his neck and tears streamed down her cheeks.

The horse stopped and Nahanna lowered her back to the ground. Her other brother, Neowassa, soon joined them. First she hugged one, and then the other, and then did it again. After the third round of hugs Nahanna held her in his arms and said, "Weenuk sends these horses to you and your son."

"What are you talking about? I have no son!" she remarked with a puzzled look on her face.

"Not yet you don't!" He replied with sparkling eyes and a huge smile.

Her face was still confused, "What?" and her eyes got bigger than a horse's and her teeth shined like stars. She leapt through the air and wrapped her arms around her brother's neck once again, this time nearly dislocating it. She danced around leading him by his neck and she hollered to the world above.

Tom leaned against the gate and checked over the new horses closely. These were fine looking animals and he would make a handsome profit on each of them. Then he turned and watched Nellie with the visitors. He was looking at the spectacle, but still didn't have a clue as to what was going on. He knew that he had some new horses in his pasture, but he had no idea what all the commotion was about. He stood there with his hands at his sides and watched his woman hugging and dancing with two strong braves.

After a while, she stopped dancing, took her brothers by the hands and led them towards Tom. She said in her native tongue, "This is my man. The white men call him Tom. And he calls me Nellie. He treats me well and has much honor in his spirit for me and our people."

With a firm grip Neowassa grasped Tom's upper arms and shook his head in respect, catching Tom by surprise. Then it was Nahanna's turn. Tom was not used to any man gripping him in this manner and it made him a little uncomfortable. His uncertainty soon vanished when he realized their smiles represented their approval.

Excitedly, Nellie took her brothers by the hands once again and brought them over to the fire pit, where she motioned them to sit.

"I have something wonderful I must show you. Tom has showed me how to cook the most delicious foods."

She quickly ran into the cabin and brought out the fixings for pancakes. Although Tom had tried on many occasions to show her how to cook on the stove, she still insisted on cooking on the open fire. Within a very short time, everyone was enjoying pancakes and syrup. Tom was the only one who drank the coffee. He offered the others the brew, but she intervened, telling them it tasted like "horse urine." Everyone had a little chuckle.

Nellie told Tom the names of each brave, and after several attempts, she was able to make Tom understand who the men were and that the horses were a gift to both of them from Weenuk.

"Boy in belly," Nellie said as she patted her stomach with excitement. Tom still didn't understand what she was talking about. Only after she made a rocking cradle motion with both arms did he catch on.

He couldn't believe his ears. He let out a joyous whoop and joined in everyone's excitement. He instinctively wanted to hug and kiss her, but he refrained because he didn't know how her brothers would react to his actions.

"You mean, I'm gonna have a son?" Tom asked her, beaming with excitement.

Nellie never let on, but she understood his words, because she knew his thoughts. This ability had been given to her by Manitou shortly after she came to live with him. She simply nodded her head yes.

Tom's first reaction was to run into the cabin and grab his jug of hard liquor, but reason stopped him quickly. He had seen the Indians after drinking, and wanted no part of it. He would wait until after they left to celebrate his impending fatherhood.

"Well, how did they know?" he asked, after allowing everything to settle. Deep down inside, he knew there was not a prayer she would be able to explain it, no matter how long or hard she tried.

Nellie was much happier with her brothers coming to her than she was about anything else. She missed them tremendously, as well as the others from her village.

"Does this mean that you will be able to come see me more?" she asked her brothers excitedly.

"I don't know, but we shall speak to Weenuk about this and see." Nahanna replied.

She grabbed his arm and looked into his eyes lovingly, and added, "I sure hope so. I miss you and the others so much."

The rest of the afternoon she showed her brothers and the others everything she learned from Tom. She even opened a book and read a few words from it. This pleased her brothers more than anything else, and they planned to tell everyone at their village about her successes.

For the rest of the warm season both Tom and Nellie spent most of their time working with the young horses. A horse had to be broken well enough not only to ride, but also to pull either a wagon or a plow.

Harness breaking was a time-consuming task, and it often required both of them to accomplish. First they had to get the horse to accept the bit in its mouth, which was never an easy thing to do. Then they had to spend hours walking behind the horse, teaching it to follow the lead they chose for it. After countless hours of teaching the horse to rein, then they had to train the horse how to pull a wagon.

This training began by using a small lightweight wagon that could easily be pulled with one hand, while holding the reins with the other. If the horse balked, became spooked or kicked back, they let go of the wagon and let the horse walk away slowly.

When the horse became comfortable with the wagon, they connected the wagon to the harness and practiced walking around the property. After all was said and done, months of long and arduous training went into each horse.

Each morning Nellie woke up with a compulsion to empty her stomach. This was believed to be from the child moving its bowels. It took time for her body to get used to this, but it adjusted quickly. Tom also noticed that her breasts were getting larger, which he enjoyed considerably. In order to address his growing desires, they spent time after each nightly reading lesson seeking pleasure from each other's bodies.

The first families that came up river rarely saw Indians, though they knew they were watched constantly. The loggers said the Indians were not hostile, but they felt they should be avoided at all costs.

Once they reached the sharp bend in the Mattawa River, families headed over land to the south and west. They sought homes with fertile soil and land that could be easily cleared. Each family headed in a slightly different direction than the family before them. The trails they left behind left a web of deep paths from the heavy burdens their wagons, and more commonly, their backs bore.

Manitou commanded the tribes and villages to abandon their ways of providing quarters to strangers. They were not allowed to kill or steal from the settlers, since the lives of their families depended upon the few items they brought with them. If the settlers perished, others with anger in their eyes and thunder sticks of death would come.

As Nellie's belly became larger, both Tom and she would rub her belly as they prepared for sleep.

Weenuk often watched her as she slept, and she felt his presence. It comforted her to know he still watched over her. The seed containing his spirit grew strong and often kicked in her belly.

"As you wish it, it shall be so!" The words woke her from a sound sleep. Her eyes snapped open and her body tensed. The words of Manitou returned to her. At first she thought the words clearly and often, trying to decipher their meaning. Then she let the words go and knew when the time came, she would know.

She quietly rose from her bed and walked out to the porch, gazing at the beauty before her. The night was brisk and moonless. All the stars in the universe illuminated the total darkness of the night. Barely a speck of sky was not twinkling in the vastness above. She stood in her nakedness, gently caressing her belly. The ball of motherhood was beginning to form, and its edges were well defined. She looked up at the stars and wished her son to be strong and healthy. She also hoped that he would have fair eyes and mind.

The stars twinkled above her. She sat on the front stoop and watched their beauty in awe, until the sun arose and they went to sleep. In the morning, she stood at the gate and watched the herd grazing. Each time she watched them, she felt a sense of pride in their beauty.

With the passage of time, Nellie's belly got larger and her patience decreased. Her new dresses became too snug for her to wear. Knowing her discomfort and changeable temperament, Tom rode to the trading post to buy her two large hides for dresses. She insisted that the baby should be covered with the clothes of her people, and she could make the dress herself. If it made her happy, Tom readily agreed.

The harvest was bountiful and there was excess to trade. Weenuk had allowed some of the women from Wishna-hea's village to visit, and she enjoyed their company tremendously. With each new visitor, she would spend hours showing him or her everything she had learned. Tom's ability to converse with the Indians increased slowly, and he was obviously her most prideful possession.

She now cooked on the stove, since the leaves started falling and the cold winds became strong. The fire felt good inside their cabin. The daylight was lessening, though the chores never did. The harvesting of the hay and oats took up most of the daylight hours. Her growing baby consumed much of her energy, and left little extra when the skies darkened. Her sleep was filled with dreams of days and years to come, and she tossed and turned throughout the night.

Tom was often awakened during the night by her moans and words he didn't understand. He watched silently as her eyes became sunken and her color became pale. When she first came to live with him, he often watched her sleep and said sweet things in his mind-with love filled eyes. Now his eyes were filled with concern. Each day her energy became less than the day before, and she refused to listen to his pleas for her to rest.

The stream of new settlers had ended for the year. This was a harsh land and the winters were severe. The sounds of trees being chopped echoed through the bush as the settlers prepared their winter supply of wood to warm their cabins. Most of Tom's horses were gone, and only a small number remained. The year had been prosperous, and Tom had fared well, but his concern for his woman grew with the passage of each day. He began wondering if the life that grew within her was a blessing or a curse.

Weenuk watched over his woman, for he, too, shared in Tom's concern. He sat cross-legged in front of his fire, and sweet grass filled the air. The smoke swirled about him and he was transported to the fire pit of Manitou.

They sat and spoke of many things. They spoke of the upcoming winter, the bountiful harvest and their returning to their winter home. This year the snows would be deep and game would become scarce once again. They spoke of the white settlers and their need of warm hides. The smoke of friendship passed between them often, as their conversations continued. After everything else was discussed, Weenuk finally brought about his true reason for requesting Manitou's counsel.

"Wishna-hea grows weak as the days grow short. I have sent her my strength, but she cannot accept it. I know nothing else I can do, and ask for your help, Manitou."

Manitou sat looking at his friend and saw through his earlier questions. "I have waited for you to ask, my friend. It is as I have told you. Her strength comes not from me but from the river she loves. She must once again drink its water and have the water against her skin, for the power of the river is strong and will give her strength. But you must not allow her to return to it. If she returns she will no longer wish to live in the white man's world."

Their conversation soon ended and Weenuk returned to his lodge. Manitou was wise and had always provided for his people.

Weenuk began sending riders to carry water to Wishna-hea right away. After Tom saw how well Nellie responded to it, he waited until she had gone out to play with her horses, and told her that he would be going to the trading post to get supplies. Nellie thought it was odd, since they lacked very little, but she paid little attention to his actions. He quickly loaded up a barrel into his wagon and rode off to the river, where he filled it with its magical waters. When he returned, he sent her out to the barn and told her he needed some trivial chore completed. She looked at him strangely, shrugged her shoulders and went and did as he asked.

As soon as she was outside, he loaded up the wood stove, went out into his shed and dragged in a metal watering troth. Then he proceeded to carry in bucket after bucket of water from the barrel. Some of which he put into pans and placed on the stove to heat. The rest he poured into the tub.

Nellie stood peeking out of the door and watched him carry bucket after bucket into the cabin. The strange things her man often did never ceased to amaze her, and this time she thought he had gone completely mad. It was not cold enough to have a large fire in the stove and yet smoke billowed from the chimney.

At first she thought he was making their cabin into a sweat lodge, but she knew that he had no knowledge of such things, so she just stood and watched from the concealment of the barn.

Before too long, Tom burst from the cabin door and excitedly told her to turn around. Having no idea what was going on, she did as he requested. In his back pocket, he had the sleeve of a shirt that had long been torn off and he tied it around her head, completely covering her eyes. He then led her into the cabin.

The cabin was as hot as any sweat lodge she had ever been in and he finally told her to remove the blindfold. When she uncovered her eyes the first thing she noticed was the floor nearly covered with water, and in the center of the room a tub filled with steamy hot water. She looked at him in confusion, but he reached in front of her, unbuttoned her dress and told her to get in the tub.

At first the water felt like it would burn her, then it turned warm and soothing. She slid beneath the water's surface and immediately recognized the water's source. Her man was truly the most wondrous man she had ever known. She popped up from the water in a splash. Reaching out quickly she wrapped her arms around his neck and hugged him dearly.

Soon she sat back down and absorbed the water's energy. Tom sat back in his chair, smiling broadly as he watched, receiving as much enjoyment as she did. Each time she tried to get out, he put his hands on her shoulders and insisted she remained. Throughout the day, he heated bucket after bucket of the water, and her strength slowly returned. Before the day was over, Tom finally said his silent prayer to the Spirit of the River.

Throughout the long winter, they repeated this bathing ritual every night. With each passing day, their bonds grew deeper. Weenuk was pleased with the man who shared his woman's bed.

# Chapter 12

The snows were heavy and the winter seemed endless, but just as day follows night, the cold passed and the warm winds once again swept through the lands. Both the Montagnais and the settlers shed their thick winter coats and began moving freely about. The moon of the Melting Snows had arrived at last.

Throughout the winter Tom kept the cabin warm and Nellie's tub full. With each bath, he added a new bucket of hot water, which he drew from the barrel rather than the pump. When the barrel was low, he took his wagon back to the river and cut blocks of ice. The ice was useful for many things, and it was much easier to deal with at this time of the year than water could possibly be. For the first time ever, he enjoyed the cold weather. The stove warmed the one-room cabin, while Nellie warmed his heart.

Before Tom met Nellie, he spent most of his life alone, never seeking the company of others. His horses kept him busy and he never had time to think of being alone. Now his life was full. He made every effort to please, and in return, received more pleasures than he had ever imagined. His relationship with Nellie was based on true caring and his patience with her differences was endless. He thoroughly enjoyed the pleasures and discoveries in her quest to learn. Like a sponge, she absorbed each and every piece of information.

Throughout the days and nights alike, he hunted for new things to show her. As soon as he found one thing, he began looking for another. However, what he enjoyed most was teaching her how to read. Since he was a child, he read the same three books over and over again until he knew each page by heart. He looked forward to getting another book from the trading post. He heard that some of the settlers traded their books, but he would never part with his, because for most of his life, they were his only source of enjoyment.

Not only did he share his home with Nellie, but he also shared it with an endless stream of visitors. Her friends from the village visited frequently. It was forbidden for a man to visit the woman of another, so the visitors were confined to the women of the village and her two brothers.

As was intended, each new thing that Nellie learned, she eagerly showed the other women. When they returned to the village, they taught the others the new information. Her most prideful accomplishment was her ability to read the words from Tom's books. She planned to teach the others how to read, but first, she had to learn more about the white man's ways.

When the evening meal was finished, Tom and Nellie sat and taught each other more about their languages. Nellie's endless thirst for knowledge prompted Tom's thirst for knowledge, as well. Together they learned, because they both had endless questions about each other's worlds.

Tom's comprehension of the Indian language was now adequate enough for him to grasp a basic understanding. It was routine for Nellie to ask questions in her tongue, and wait, impatiently at times, for his response. Despite her encouragement, he didn't quite grasp speaking her language. However, by using one and two word phrases, combined with gestures, he made himself understand.

She gained the greatest understanding of his language by reading the words in his books. Through this repetition her knowledge of his language far surpassed his greatest expectations. He often wondered why her people never learned to write. It would have been so much easier for him to learn, if only he could see the words and sentences in print.

When Nellie's friends visited, the women frequently passed comments between themselves just to watch Tom's reactions. They always encouraged him to talk to them, and when their comments were of a personal nature, they laughed when he became embarrassed.

For the first time in his adult life, he shared his company with others. The more often the women visited, the less bashful he became. When the women came with their children, Tom often took them to the barn. He always thought of something new to amuse them with, and he took great delight in spending time with the children. He found that it was much easier to communicate with kids. His interest in children was quickly reported back to Weenuk, who then shared it with Manitou. They were both pleased that Tom enjoyed children.

On one of his trips to the trading post, Tom picked up several decks of cards. He was very excited to show Nellie and her friends how to play. The first problem he encountered was teaching them the numbers. He started by teaching them a game he had learned as a child. It was called War. War without bloodshed was always enjoyable, and the game was learned quickly.

The women thoroughly enjoyed learning how to play games. In their village, they never had time to participate in games. Only children and men were allowed such luxuries, and discovering a game that they could actually play, was very exciting to them. The tiny cabin became a beacon of laughter and enjoyment for all those who visited.

Playing cards was considered a good thing. Not only was it entertaining, but it was also a fun way to teach the Indians the white man's numbers. The spare decks that Tom gave out were soon worn out from the near constant use.

As the winter progressed, Nellie's belly got bigger. The larger it grew, the more often her temper flared. Even the horses shied away when she came into the barn. Her bed became uncomfortable; her nipples often leaked; and her bladder gained a mind of its own. To top it all off, her dress no longer fit.

When Tom smiled or laughed at her awkwardness, she threw anything that she could get her hands on. After living through her pregnancy, fatherhood would definitely be a welcome change.

When the big day finally arrived, two old women from her village stayed through the night and chased Tom away. Birthing wasn't something men took well, so Tom stayed with the horses. When he finished cleaning the stalls, he added a top layer of saw dust that he picked up from the mill. He also oiled all of the harnesses and saddles. When all of the necessary chores were finished, he picked up a brush and began brushing one horse after another.

This was a luxury that he hadn't allowed himself for more years than he could remember. The only time he ever brushed out a horse was when he was expecting a potential buyer. Today this was totally a labor of love. While he mindlessly brushed out the horses, he told them all of his troubles. He had forgotten just how astute they were at listening. The last time he remembered doing this was when he was a kid. He'd almost forgotten that there had been enjoyment in his childhood. As he brushed the horses, more and more of his childhood memories returned. Some weren't pleasant, but on this day, he tried to remember the good times.

The contractions ripped through Nellie's abdomen as the infant prepared her for birth. Sweat poured from her body and she bit down hard on the leather strap.

"Push," the old women repeated again and again. Each time she pushed, the baby moved closer and closer. From somewhere deep inside her, a scream worked its way through her lungs as the baby's head emerged. The old women were proficient and the birth went well.

Manitou breathed life strongly into the infant's lungs, and like the call of the rooster, the sounds of the infant's cries broke through the morning air.

"Oh, Jesus!" exclaimed Tom, as he heard the cry and ran straight for the cabin. When he threw the door open, he saw Nellie holding a small bundle on her breast. Her eyes sparkled and they were focused on the suckling infant. Slowly Tom walked up to her, and their eyes met. They exchanged a universe of thoughts.

The child suckled contentedly as Tom looked down at his slick black hair. The baby's head was not much larger than Tom's fist. He knelt down at the side of Nellie's bed, took her hand in his and pressed it to his lips. Pride washed over him as he watched the baby move against her. He looked into her eyes and her smile told him that everything was fine. He reached out, touched the infant's head and looked back at Nellie. She lifted the baby from her breast and held him in her hands, almost as an offering to Tom.

Nervously, he took the baby in his hands, held him out and gazed at the tiny helpless form. The baby's hair was black and his eyes were blue. His skin was as wrinkled as an old man, and his hands were the smallest things he had ever seen. He slowly brought the baby against his chest and wrapped his arms around the tiny figure. The look in Tom's eyes said it all. They grew large as the infant wiggled against him. Suddenly, panic swept over him and he handed the baby back to Nellie. She looked at the two of them, and she was proud to be alive.

This was truly a moment they would remember for the rest of their lives. Their love would be shared with this bundle of joy forever. Tom pressed his lips to Nellie's cheek and held her face in his hands. "I love you!" he spoke softly.

The old women watched with great satisfaction as the new parents discovered all the wondrous parts of their new baby. After giving the family adequate time together, the women chased Tom out. After all, there were plenty of "woman" things to be done.

The wise Snow Owl watched from the roof of the barn, and upon seeing Tom emerge happy from the cabin, it spread its wings and flew off to tell Manitou of the birth. As the owl flew high above, Tom didn't even notice the mighty bird because he was so preoccupied with the birth of his new son. He wanted to saddle up a horse and ride to the trading post, but it was the middle of the night, so he had to be content with telling the news to the horses and cats that lived in the barn.

By the time the old women reached their village, the news of Wishna-hea's baby had already been spread everywhere.

Apparently, Weenuk was so excited by the news, he told everyone about it. The women enjoyed describing the details of the birth, as well as the reactions of the new parents. Tom's approval was discussed and discussed again. It appeared that each woman had a totally different view on the subject, and each one enjoyed telling it to anyone who would listen. The village became a beehive of chatter.

Gifts of toys and dolls were collected and each of the women wanted to be present when the gifts were given. For once, the men of the tribe were left behind and nearly every woman, including their children, converged on the small cabin.

Neither Tom nor Nellie was prepared for the surprise visit of more than twenty women and their children. When the women arrived, they lit the fire pit and prepared dishes to celebrate the baby's arrival. Tom decided to leave the chaos of the cabin behind him, and he headed to the river with his fishing pole. He was amazed at his luck. It appeared that even the Spirit of the River was in a giving mood.

It was more than a week before Tom and Nellie actually had the baby to themselves. By then, Nellie was well over the traumas of birthing, and she blossomed in her delight. The child's suckling took energy from her, but the Spirit of the River kept her revitalized. The daily bathing became ritualistic, and Tom provided the water without fail. If the power from the river kept his woman healthy and strong, then it must be good for his son, too. So now he kept two barrels of water full at all times.

The planting season was coming soon, so Tom agreed to let Nellie show her friends how to use the horse and plow to till their soil. After further discussion, he also agreed to lend them his team and plow, since they had given them so much.

When the women arrived for their instruction, they were so excited to learn about the white man's way of planting. Before they began, Nellie invited everyone in for pancakes, which was a total treat for them all. While she entertained her guests and tended the baby, Tom grained, watered and hayed the horses. By the time he was finished, his coffee was nice and strong and his plate was heaped with pancakes.

While the women talked excitedly, he gobbled down his food and then headed back outside to hook up the horse and plow. When everything was ready, he let Nellie show off her stuff. It didn't take long for her to get to work. She stood behind the plow with the reins in her hand, and with a quick twitch, the horse was off. While the plow dug in deeply, she heard everyone's oooh's and aaah's. The women watched closely. Nellie expertly turned the horse and plow around, and began her second pass, then a third, and finally a fourth. After a considerable time, she stopped and called the women in close to begin their individual lessons.

By the end of the day, the women had plowed up nearly half of the field. Tom hadn't planned on reseeding his pasture, but since they did the work, it seemed like a good idea. The following day they finished the pasture and dug the garden.

After both Nellie and Tom were satisfied with the women's abilities, he loaded up the plow, tied the horse to his wagon, and drove to the village. The women sat excitedly in the back, all chattering while they marveled over the plow. Their harvest would be large this season, and all of their people would prosper. No longer would they have to worry about starvation during the long season of deep snows and brutal cold.

The spring turned to summer and Allumette Island once again took on its summer residents. The fish were large, and with the coming of the dragonflies, the black flies finally subsided. Life carried on, just as it had for hundreds of years before. The people of the land lived in harmony with Mother Earth and Father Sky.

The white settlers once again began to trickle in. The numbers increased and they pushed farther and deeper into the hunting grounds of the Montagnais and Nipissing. Cabins began sprouting up on the banks of the rivers and lakes. The settlers chopped the trees, cleared the land, and tilled the soil. The face of the lands of the great Manitou was scarred, and would never again be as it was intended.

There was so much to learn, and Tom became an astute teacher. Nellie did not allow him to show his cooking skills to the women of the village. She knew the men in her village would forbid their women to continue visiting if they started asking the men to do any cooking. So Tom taught Nellie how to prepare his favorite dishes, then she, in turn, showed the women how to do the food preparation.

The people of Chief du Fond's village were learning much about the ways of the white man. The other villages watched closely and saw the wisdom of Manitou's words. In order to understand the white man, they had to understand their God, and in order to live among them, they had to learn their ways.

It was time for the other villages to learn this knowledge, so Chief du Fond and the elders planned a pow-wow in their village. The Montagnais were a proud people and they were anxious to share their successes with others. Their gardens were well fertilized and their crops grew like weeds. The gardens of the surrounding villages paled by comparison. Now each lodge in the village had a kerosene lantern inside, and they all cooked the white man's food in great abundance.

"Nellie, why don't you go back to your village for the pow-wow?" Tom asked while they ate their midday meal.

She shook her head in silence, though in her heart she begged to go. "It is not permitted." Her words were barely above a whisper.

Tom had never questioned why she had come to live with him, though the question never really left his mind. Why was he selected above all others to share his life with this beautiful and wonderful woman? Why was he so readily accepted by all of the people of her village, when the Indians avoided contact with the whites? Even the Indians that lived next to the trading post avoided even the slightest physical contact with the post's agents and the loggers.

Nellie sat silently. She longed to once again walk in her village and see all of her family and friends. The village would be filled with all kinds of excitement. She wished she could watch the games of lacrosse and visit with others from different villages. She wanted to share all of the new things she learned from Tom. After all, she was the one who discovered them all. For the first time, she felt resentful.

She thought about her river and swimming in its depths. She thought about the gorge, in its breathless magnificence, even though it still harbored many of her fears.

Like the raging waters, the buried memories returned—the roaring of the Bear and the screams of the Mohawks and their horses. These memories haunted her. She shuddered at the thought of the headless body of her captor, and the blood that covered her body. Her thoughts also shifted to Weenuk and the power that he released through his eyes. Her thoughts lingered to the last night she spent with Weenuk. The nagging thoughts continued to spin in her head.

She wanted to be that child who swam in the cool waters and played with the fish. She loved the river's water, but knew should could not return there. Before long, a smile returned to her face, and she knew that she was living the life that Manitou intended.

Like the loggers before them, the settlers were interested in changing the land. They cut the trees, made their homes and turned the bush into fields. The longer the sun stayed in the sky, the more trees they cut down. Still, their numbers increased, as word of the pioneer's successes reverberated back to the towns and villages. Rumors that upper and lower Canada were becoming united, also fueled the fires of exploration.

The settlers spread along the banks of the Mattawa River to Lake Talon, Trout, Nobosing, and Wistiwasin. They traveled up the Thessalon deep into the lands of the Mississauga. They spread far and quickly. The rivers soon became highways for the white man. Men from the new country's government began making treaties with the Indian Nations. Soon the Indians and their ways would be considered obstacles that must be overcome.

Manitou watched with saddened eyes as the settlers pushed on. The animals of the bush looked for solitude and moved from their lands. Iron trails in the South and East brought more men to cut trees. In fact, the loggers soon clogged the rivers with the trees that once sheltered the lands and were home to many animals.

The families came with the barest of essentials. They were finally realizing their hopes and dreams. The lands were vast and the earth was fertile. This allowed them a wonderful opportunity to live off of the land and prosper.

Nellie's cradleboard fit snugly on her back as she hoed the garden. The sun beat down upon her and she wiped the perspiration from her brow. The garden was large and because of the fertilizer, the weeds grew even faster than the plants.

She shrugged her shoulders in pace with her quiet chanting and the baby whimpered softly. The whimpers soon turned to coos of contentment and Nellie smiled.

"You don't have a name yet, but you have my heart. Everything I do, I do for you and our people." She spoke softly to the child.

Tom's business continued to grow and he constantly looked for new horses to trade. His fairness earned him respect from both the Indians and the white man. He liked training his horses because trained horses brought in much higher profits. The training ring's ground was pounded flat from continual use. Horses that were trained to pull plows were worth their weight in gold, but they also required a lot more time and effort.

There just didn't seem to be enough hours in the day for Tom to finish all of his tasks. He thought about the hay and oats that had to be harvested. He thought about his large herd and the land that had to be cleared, tilled and seeded. The summer promised to be long. His days began before the rooster crowed and only stopped when the sky was totally black. The evening meal became the family's only time to enjoy each other's company, and all too soon, an exhausted sleep filled their evenings.

"Next year you'll walk behind me," Nellie thought to herself. "Then I'll make you your own hoe, so you'll learn not to be lazy." The thought of her son as a toddler, struggling to hold his balance while walking beside her, brought a huge smile to her face.

"I'll teach you to talk to the horses," her conversation continued. "And you'll ride like an Indian. I will teach you to talk and walk with the spirits, so that you can understand the teachings of our ancestors. Tom will teach you the ways of trading and you will someday take over for him, when we grow old and gray."

The thought of getting old did not amuse her at all. She continued, "No. Maybe someday you'll become chief." Then she remembered that her son would not grow up in the world of her people, so she quickly changed her thoughts.

# Chapter 13

The white men called it Indian summer. The days were warm and the nights were mild. The leaves of the bush started turning red and yellow and every shade in between.

Nellie enjoyed taking long rides with Tom and the baby into the bush just to enjoy the beauty of the land. She often thought about riding towards her village and showing Tom her favorite places in the world, but she knew it was forbidden, so she erased the thought from her mind.

The workload slowed as the warm weather continued. Tom finished building a new storage barn for hay and grain, which had been cut three times already. The barn was nearly bursting with the harvest. This year he had more hay and grain than he could possibly use, and he planned to sell some of it to the settlers who didn't have time to plant their own.

Since the settlers became more numerous in the area, Tom kept more horses on his land. Last year he only had five horses, but this year he had sixteen. They were all strong stock and could pull either a wagon or a plow. With the longer season, he had time to finish training them all.

He had ten stalls in the barn, but he liked keeping the horses in open areas, so they could come and go as the weather allowed. He pounded heavy rings into the logs and tied up the horses during the deep snows and severely cold temperatures.

Tom looked forward to winter. He had a new family, and he never felt so at ease. He never thought much of babies, but this baby was the center of his world. He figured by the end of winter he'd have to put in a new board floor in their cabin, so the young boy could crawl around on his own.

The autumn ended abruptly and snow began to fall. It hadn't rained much in the summer, but it looked like the winter would make up for it. Nearly every day more snow fell. At first, the snow was fun. Tom hadn't had a snowball fight in more years than he could remember. Everyday when they went outside, Nellie started a snowball fight with him. She had a way of bringing out the kid in him, and at twenty-eight, he felt the kid inside was entitled to return once in a while.

As the snows continued, travel became more difficult, and the deeper the snows became, the fewer the visitors came. It seemed like everyone had nestled in for the long winter that lay ahead. Everything was covered in white. On the few nights when it wasn't snowing, the stars and moonlight lit up the sky, creating a snowy glow.

During this hard winter, Father Bruel, the local preacher, came down with a cough that made talking almost impossible. Honey and whiskey were no remedy for his ailment. His cough came from deep within his lungs, and each cough brought up a small amount of blood nearly each time. He called off his lessons with the Indians and figured that he would resume them in the spring.

He had been pleased with his progress. Since his lessons began, he believed he was changing some of the Indians into believers. Even the old Indians seemed to listen now. When they first started coming, they grumbled so loudly it distracted the youngsters. Now they listened silently, though their scowls never left their faces.

Teaching the Indians religion first meant teaching them how to speak English, even though Father Bruel preferred speaking French. Most of the loggers and new settlers spoke English, so the French would only confuse the Indians. He started by teaching them the Lord's Prayer.

Father Bruel's coughing sapped all of his strength, and the slightest effort left him gasping for breath. The agents at the trading post insisted that he stay in the back room, where they could keep an eye on him. Only when his pale complexion began to take on a gray casting, did they realize that they needed to call in a doctor. The problem was, there were no doctors within nearly thirty miles. Before they could fetch a doctor, the preacher would be dead. They should have sent someone out sooner, but they really thought his condition would have improved by now.

At first, they scoffed at an Indian's suggestion to call out the Medicine Man, Weenuk. But he soon became their only option. They sent a rider out to the Montagnais village and told Weenuk that they needed his medicine as quickly as possible.

Since daybreak, more than a foot of snow fell. There was no relief in sight. It didn't take Weenuk long to prepare for his trip to the trading post. He gathered his medicines and spiritual tools and packed them all safely into a pouch. He then summoned his drummer and a singer, who acted as his assistants. He would have preferred to have Wishna-hea accompany him, but he knew that was out of the question.

Within twenty minutes of the rider's arrival, the small party headed out into the raging storm. The winds howled and the trees bent wildly. It wasn't long before the horses tired from the snow drifts, which were up to their bellies. The trail that led to the trading post became impassable, so the small group headed to another trail through the pines. Although this trail was much longer, it offered some protection from the storm. Normally the ride would have taken no more than a couple of hours, but they were approaching three hours, and they were not even half way there yet.

The snow and winds continued to howl as the four men pressed on. Weenuk believed that the fury of the storm was a bad omen, but he said nothing to the others. Even the great pines offered little protection. Out of the corner of his eye, he saw something move. He signaled the others to stop, while he scanned the bush to find the source of the movement. In the distance off to his left, he saw a large brown form standing near the trees. At first he thought it was a cabin, because it was too large for an animal. Perhaps they could seek shelter until the storm had passed. Then his eyes adjusted to the snow, and standing before him was the Great Bear of Manitou.

The others held their heads low to shield their eyes from the blinding snow and saw nothing. Weenuk sat up straight and he hailed the Great Bear. His thoughts pierced through the storm.

"Oh Great Bear, why do you come to me this day? Is this the day I join my ancestors?" Weenuk sent out his thoughts, but they were quickly carried away by the wind. Again, he shouted and still no answer was heard.

The Great Bear vanished, and he wondered if his eyes were playing tricks on him. It was not like Manitou to ignore his questions. Even the trees groaned from the wind and snow. Still the storm persisted. They pressed on.

Before too long, the Great Bear appeared again. Only this time it was the bear that spoke.

"My old friend, we have shared company for a long time, and I have grown accustomed to your ways. I have taught you to be the giver of life, but now you are becoming the messenger of death, and I cannot prevent it."

Weenuk responded with his thoughts, "Then strike me down and let the others live. For I am an old man, and I have seen many things."

"You have been summoned to the bed of the man who preaches. Just as with other sachems, you must go and do what you can to heal others. You must go to him. It is what you must do."

As the Bear's words ended, the winds diminished and the snow stopped. Weenuk said nothing, but kicked his horse's sides and encouraged the cold and tired beast onward.

Within a short time they reached the trading post. Never before had Weenuk set foot in a square lodge of trees, and one of the others had to show him how to use the doorknob.

The walls of the trading post were lined with shelves. Barrels were stacked and crude shelving formed isles in the building. The heat from the stove kept the post warm and the coats were hung from pegs at the door. The Indian messenger that had been sent to fetch Weenuk, took Weenuk's heavy bear coat and hung it upon the peg. The others hung their coats and watched for Weenuk's reactions, as did everyone else.

Weenuk looked around the room, absorbing all of its contents. He looked at the white men who were staring at him.

"Take me to the one that preaches!" he said in his native tongue to the Indian messenger.

He and the others were lead through the post and into the back room, where Father Bruel lay on a bed covered with blankets. His coughs echoed against the wooden walls and his eyes remained shut. Even though the preacher was gravely sick, Weenuk felt his emotions. Both men came from opposing worlds, but they both held strong spiritual beliefs.

Weenuk placed his hand upon the ailing man's forehead and felt his raging fever. "Take off these robes and bring me snow!" he barked out to the others.

One of the agents moved to protest, but the oldest one put his hand upon his shoulder and said, "Let him be. Maybe this old Medicine Man knows something we don't." Then they all watched from a distance in silence.

Of the three agents, none of them had seen the magic of a Medicine Man. They knew that the Indians who came to the post both feared and respected Weenuk. In fact, they considered him nearly God like. While the agents were waiting for him to arrive at their post, they were told of his powers over the animals in the bush, especially the bears. When they heard about how he had transformed himself into a bear that was larger than a house, they outwardly scoffed. Though deep inside, they were apprehensive of the possible powers he may be able to unleash.

They watched as Weenuk took the clothing from the preacher and rubbed snow over his entire body. Suddenly, a coughing attack brought the preacher to a sitting position. The Indian messenger moved quickly and put a bucket under the preacher's mouth. The bucket already had several inches of bloody mucus in it. Weenuk dipped his fingers into the bloody mess, and then brought them to his nose. He smelled deeply. The blood smelled of death.

The four Indian families who lived near the trading post came in as soon as they heard of Weenuk's arrival. They wanted to see his magic with their own eyes.

Healing wasn't something that could be done with others present, so Weenuk sent everyone from the room, except his two helpers. The drummer began his steady beat, and the other man began his chant. The pair had done this countless times, but this time, Weenuk's eyes projected an intensity they had not seen before.

He chanted and called out for the healing spirits of all who had passed before him. First he called out to his animal spirit, the Great Bear of the North. Then he called to the spirits of his father and his grandfather. He summoned his most powerful healing spirits, and asked if they would summon the others who could help him chase the evil spirit of death away from the preacher. Together with the spirits, Weenuk began his journey into the center of Mother Earth.

When they reached their destination in the Underworld, Weenuk saw the spirit of the preacher. He was struggling with an unseen host, who refused to reveal himself to Weenuk.

"Reveal yourself to me, if you dare!" Weenuk demanded of the hidden spirit. "Release him and allow his spirit to remain with his body!"

"Do not speak to me in that tone, you evil pagan priest!" The spirit hollered out to him.

"I wish no harm to come to him, and I appeal to your love for him. He teaches my people of your ways and of your God. Because of this, I call not only to your God, but also to mine."

"Your powers are a joke and your God is but a child. Leave us now, and let us take his spirit with us. We offer him peace and happiness."

"But you offer him death, not peace."

"Is there not peace in death? Old Man, you should know that, for you have knocked on its door for ages now! Stand aside and let me move on. I have matters that need my attention, and I tire of these games."

The Evil Spirit's temper was beginning to flair and he finally revealed himself to Weenuk. Never before had Weenuk met this Evil One. He didn't know how to convince him of his detriment to the preacher or how to trick him into releasing the preacher's spirit.

Weenuk's strength alone could not battle this powerful enemy. He needed the strength and wisdom of his ancestors and animal spirit helpers. The more power he required, the louder his chanting became.

"It is not your power I question." Weenuk continued. "I chant only for your mercy, since this man has done nothing to offend you."

The battle for the preacher's soul ensued. Weenuk was determined to keep the preacher's spirit among those of the world walkers.

Day became night, and night became day. The battle raged on. The others listened hard as the sounds of the drums and chants radiated from behind the door. The agents passed a jug of liquor between them and several times offered it to the Indians. However, the Indians dared not to take a drink in the presence of Weenuk.

Again the sunset and darkness covered the land. Weenuk's strength and powers had begun to wane. The spirits battled back and forth. Weenuk and his ancestors had great strength, but the Evil One's powers were as vast as the universe.

It was well past midnight when the battle finally ended. The Evil Spirit defeated Weenuk. The chanting and drumming stopped. Regardless of how hard he tried, Weenuk's healing spirits could not maintain the upper hand, and in the end, the preacher's spirit was whisked away.

Weenuk lowered his head and used his arms to support his weight. He couldn't remember ever expending this much energy to fight an evil spirit. He remained kneeling on the floor until he was able to regain his strength. After he was strong enough to stand, he just turned and stared at the door. He remembered that he was the reason why everyone on the other side of the door was here. His pride was not at stake, but his belief in his ancestor's spirits was on trial here, and he had failed.

The Indians' horses had been fed, sheltered and were well rested. As Weenuk and his party mounted their horses, they heard mock chanting from one of the post's agents. The others laughed hardily at Weenuk's beliefs and strange methods. The Indians rode back to their village in silence.

The trail was nearly clear and the horses rode quickly. They traveled more than half the distance when one of the Indians spotted a moose at the tree line. At first he thought his eyes were playing tricks on him. Then he shook his head and looked again. "Look!" he shouted.

The moose was pure white. The Indians did not raise their bows or arrows, and they stood transfixed by the animal. Its fur was as white as the snow, but its eyes were as red as blood. It stood its ground and snorted, pawing at the snow-covered Earth. Its eyes sought contact. Weenuk turned his horse and faced the moose squarely.

"I am Weenuk, Sachem of the Montagnais. Who is it that seeks my counsel?"

"My coat is pure, as is my heart and spirit. I seek no counsel. I am only here to see you with my eyes. I have heard of your greatness and your powers. I wish to walk beside you and share your knowledge. But for this, we have no time."

"Then why do you approach me? Are you from the land of spirits? It's only there where Manitou will allow an animal of your color."

Weenuk thought for a moment, then continued, "Are you here to take me to my ancestors?"

"It is not time, my friend. But when I return to you, you shall ride upon my back, and I shall be honored to carry you to your ancestors and His home."

"Then I shall await your return and prepare for the long journey." Weenuk kicked his horse's side and led the band away. The winds of death were coming. Neither chants nor potions could prevent their arrival.

Lying on her back, Nellie stared into the darkness. Her dream had been horrific. She dreamed that she walked once again through her village and the bodies of her friends were scattered on the ground, half covered with snow. They lay in a puddle of their own blood, as if some massacre had taken place. There were no arrows or even bullet holes in the corpses, yet blood poured from their mouths. Their dogs were standing over their bodies, growling viciously as she approached. The fire pit was half covered with snow, and no embers burned.

Silently they slept. Their spirits had long since passed. Panic rose in her body and she ran towards Weenuk's lodge. Her feet were mired in mud. The harder she struggled, the deeper she sank. Terror wrenched through her whole body. When she looked down she noticed that it wasn't mud that gripped her feet, but it was a pool of blood. She cried out desperately for Weenuk, but she didn't hear a sound.

Sweat poured from her body and her eyes filled with tears. She snapped up quickly and sat upon her bed, struggling to adjust her eyes to the darkness. Frantically, she reached out to feel Tom and her baby.

Tom groaned as her hands reached out. She grabbed at him desperately, trying to feel the life inside him. Relieved when she felt his warmth, she reached into the baby's cradle and covered him once again.

She slowly got up from bed, making sure she did not wake Tom or the baby. She slipped her dress over her head and looked around the room. The full moon was reflected in the newly fallen snow, and its shimmering light filled the room. She added three logs to the fire, then walked to the door and opened it. The cold night rushed in, so she stepped back into the cabin to retrieve her coat and mukluks. Silently, she walked back to the door. The old hinges squeaked as she slid outside.

"Manitou, what is the meaning of my dreams? Why were my people dead, and why do I dream of this?"

Her coat kept her warm, yet she shivered. The universe of stars twinkled brightly above her and she gazed out passed their beauty.

"Manitou, oh Manitou, I call out to you. Come talk to me and tell me this dream cannot be so!"

After a few moments of silence, she heard a voice. "Our world has changed my little one, for this is our destiny. I can do nothing to stop it. I have sent you into the future, for you are our future and must remain where you are."

"If this is what lies ahead for our people, let me go home, so I can die like the others. Don't let me be the last to survive, for that would be worse than death. Let me die and forget my dreams, and come home to my ancestors."

"No, my child. You have become a giver of life, not only to your son, but also to your people. You must now become isolated from them forever. Until the cloud of death passes, you will not be permitted to see the others from your village. You must remain strong. The child who suckles your breast is the hope of your people, and you must shelter him from all harm."

"I would gladly give my life for my child and my people. If I cannot see my people, isn't that death in itself?"

"The future of life is in your hands, so treat it wisely!"

The conversation ended. Nellie looked out into the vastness of the stars and sadness overwhelmed her. She fell to her knees and then flat upon the snow. Her tears melted holes deep in the snowy blanket. She sobbed and cried, using the snow to muffle her sounds.

The baby's cries startled her, and she got back on her feet. She brushed the snow from her thick coat and wiped her eyes. "It's only cries of hunger," she mumbled to herself. She then breathed a sigh of relief and smiled. Her child would be saved!

Before she entered the cabin, she turned towards the direction of her village. She stared off into the distance, wishing her dream wouldn't become reality. She promised herself that she would soon teach her young son about her ancestor's ways.

When she went inside, the baby was sitting up with tears running down his cheeks. She scooped him up quickly and clutched him to her breast. She rocked him gently back and forth, trying to soothe him, as well as herself.

She cradled him for more than an hour before Tom woke up. He rubbed his eyes and noticed that Nellie was wearing her coat and boots. In fact, she was standing in a puddle of melted snow and mud. He rubbed his eyes again.

She smiled while the baby laughed, saying, "I've decided his name. It's going to be Jimmy. He's going to be Jimmy forever."

"What do you mean, Nellie? Why do you have your coat on?" Tom asked groggily. "Wait a minute. Did you just say that you named the baby Jimmy?"

Without waiting for an answer he continued his questions. "Why is he getting a name now? You said he couldn't get a name until he was two. Did I sleep longer than I thought or something?"

With a scowl on her face, she retorted, "Now don't you start bothering me. I like that name. Jimmy suits him just fine. That's going to be his name and I don't want to hear anymore about it."

Tom's heart leapt with joy because he had been thinking of naming the boy Jimmy for many months now. He couldn't be more pleased! He gave Nellie a big squeeze, then he headed outside to use the outhouse.

During the following weeks, Tom asked Nellie why none of her friends came to visit any more. She just avoided his questions. He didn't press the issue because he figured there must be a logical reason. What really surprised him though was her attitude. She seemed to change over night. She began waiting on him hand and foot. Whenever he made the slightest move or gesture, she came rushing to see what he needed. At first, he found it amusing, but eventually the novelty wore off. He was content with the old Nellie and didn't want her to act any differently.

A cold snap entered the area and the temperatures plummeted. Tom had to chop holes in the ice to allow the horses to drink. He used a heavy metal bar to chop through the thick ice. He made sure the holes were large enough so the horses could drink their fill before the ice froze back over.

With the work load easing due to the cold weather, Tom finally had a chance to put the wooden floor in the cabin. When he finished, he wondered why he hadn't done it sooner. The cabin immediately became warmer, and little Jimmy was able to crawl all over the place.

# Chapter 14

The tribal council sat around Weenuk's fire pit, waiting for the meeting to begin. Since the temperatures outside were extremely cold, they used the fire for warmth. Dressed in their heavy bearskins, they huddled close together ready to discuss their future.

First, they passed around the smudge pot, so each tribal member could cleanse his or her own spirit with smoke from the sacred herbs. Then they tossed cedar and tobacco into the fire to draw out the sacredness of the flames. The mood became somber, as the Spirit of the Sacred Fire manifested itself and began to exchange energy with the council members.

Weenuk stood and began chanting, while holding his hands up to the sky. "Hey-ya, Hey-ya, Hey-ya . . ." He droned on in a monotone chant. His drummer followed the fluctuations of his voice. He sent out a petition to the ancestors, who were now required at the sacred fire.

He waved his sweet-grass braid over his head and continued to chant. The smoke from the fire mingled with the sweet grass, creating a spiral. Soon the spiral was so large that it consumed the entire lodge.

Weenuk spoke and asked if the ancestors would make themselves visible for all to see, but they declined. A new tribal member had been added to the council, and they wanted to know more about this woman, before they would show themselves.

One member had coughed himself to death, so they had to replace his seat with a new member. It seemed that nearly all of the council members had developed the cough, as did many of the villagers. The purpose of this council meeting was to figure out how to handle this unknown sickness. The Chief held his hand up signaling silence.

He spoke to the ancestors, "We welcome you to our lodge and give thanks for your time."

The sacred pipe of friendship was passed around the lodge. Each member held it above his or her head, giving a nod to signify his or her thanks to the ancestors. The ancestors sat along side each of the members, but only Weenuk and the Chief could see them.

One ancestor whispered, "The Black Bird of Death has come into our lands and spreads like wildfire. Manitou has told us of this. It has been said that we have only seen the first of our people to die. There will be many deaths."

Weenuk added solemnly, "I have seen the White Moose and his eyes were angry. I agree with our ancestors. Our future does not look good. Only the strongest of our people will survive."

A long silence followed. No one expected this. The members sat with blank expressions on their faces, hands hanging at their sides. The reality of their dreams set in and their future looked bleak.

"How long will the cloud of death remain with our people? How many shall die?" The oldest woman asked.

"The cloud of death will remain with us until the snowflakes die in spring." Weenuk answered.

No one moved or spoke. A single cough broke the silence. Each member began looking at the others. "Weenuk, surely you can mix up some herbs and cure us. Save our people. You are the strongest healer of any Algonquin. This is something you must do."

"I cannot, nor can Manitou. This coughing sickness is not like any other. My medicines do nothing. All we can do is wait and see who is strong enough to survive. After the sickness leaves, we must rebuild." Weenuk replied.

Jimmy turned two years old and was an endless chatterbox.

Nellie taught him how to use the ancient language of the Spirit to talk to the animals. Whenever his parents were busy with their chores, he talked to all of the animals in the barnyard. Of all the animals in the barnyard, he enjoyed talking to the rooster the most.

When he spoke to the rooster, he knelt down and propped his chin up so he could look directly into the bird's eyes. He spent countless hours in deep conversation with the rooster. When Tom asked him why he didn't just pick the rooster up to talk to him, Jimmy happily informed him that the rooster didn't want to be picked up.

"He likes the ground." Jimmy explained.

After Nellie was satisfied with Jimmy's progress in speaking to the animals, she brought him into the bush, away from the distractions of the yard, to begin his next lesson. She began teaching him how to communicate with the Spirits of the Bush.

"Jimmy, I want you to look at that tree." He knew that he was getting another lesson, because this was the only time his mother would speak to him in her native language.

"Just like your rooster and the other animals have spirits that want to talk to you, so do the trees and everything else in the bush."

Jimmy looked at her with sparkling eyes and asked, "Can I talk to trees, too?"

"Yes, Jimmy, and what's even better, is that they have been waiting to talk to you, too!" Jimmy could barely contain his excitement.

"Instead of just looking at the bark and leaves of the tree, I want you to look deep inside the tree, just like I taught you to do with the rooster and your other friends in the barnyard."

Jimmy scrunched his eyes and turned and twisted his head. Nellie waited and watched as he went through his antics. When she was sure he was tuning in, she continued, "You are doing really good. Now I want you to tell the tree, just like you do your rooster, that you are happy to meet him."

Jimmy concentrated with all of his energy. Nellie watched

his facial expressions with amusement and pride, as he sent out his message for the first time.

"Can you feel the tree listening?"

"Yes."

"Is he saying anything back to you?"

"No."

"Now I want you to tell him that you want to talk with him, and tell me what he says."

After a short time Jimmy replied, "He wants to talk to me."

"He knew you would be coming to talk to him. Trees are very wise, and they know many things that we don't."

"How come he's so smart?"

"Trees are very old. They are much older than people, but unlike people they watch things really good. They know that Mother Earth knows everything, and they listen and learn from Her."

"What's she say to them?"

"Well, she told the trees that someday you would be born, and that you would come and talk to them."

"They knew I was coming?" His eyes were beaming with joy. "Wow!"

Nellie knew of the pure delight he gained from this.

"See if you can hear what he is saying to you now."

After a few minutes Jimmy got up and walked over to the tree and wrapped his little arms around the huge trunk. "He wants a hug!"

Nellie was filled with a huge sense of pride. He had learned his lesson well.

It was soon time for Jimmy to get his first riding lesson. Both Tom and Nellie were excited. Nellie insisted that he ride without a saddle, and after a lengthy debate, Tom reluctantly gave in.

Nellie wove a saddle blanket for Jimmy during the winter and kept it hidden from Tom. She wanted to surprise both of her men at the same time. When she put it on the pony's back, Tom commented, "That is one fine looking blanket."

The snow was finally melting and the ring was fairly barren. Jimmy's mount was a pony that Tom picked up a short time before from one of the farmers. The pony was black and had a white streak from her left eye to the tip of her nose. Opposing white socks earned her the name of Miss Match. Her disposition was like a lamb, and she had magical eyes.

As soon as Nellie put Jimmy on the pony's back, he instinctively grabbed on tightly to the pony's mane. Nellie slowly let go and walked beside the pony with her arms held out in case she needed to catch him. Tom led the group around the ring. Before they were halfway around, Jimmy held his balance and was having a ball. He bounced excitedly on the pony's back.

Miss Match was equally content with her new rider, and took good care of him. Their bond was instant. Another trip around the ring and Nellie reluctantly stood off to the side and watched. She held her fists nervously to her mouth. Jimmy, however, quickly mastered his new skill. A huge smile was plastered all over his face as he rode around in circles. Tom was delighted by his son's riding ability. He hated to agree, but Nellie was right—Jimmy didn't need a saddle right now.

Jimmy's love for Miss Match began the first moment he laid his eyes on her. It didn't take long for him to grasp the basic riding commands—right, left, stop, go, walk, and run. Within a couple of short weeks, Nellie began taking him from the ring to short rides down the trail. Miss Match always maintained her manners and carried Jimmy safely.

The two became the best of friends. When it stormed, Jimmy climbed into Miss' Match's stall, and spent countless hours talking to her in his usual, non-stop manner. Tom often wondered if the pony actually understood, because at times, the conversations appeared to be two sided.

When Nellie worked in the garden or out in the pastures with the other horses, Jimmy and Miss Match entertained each other for hours. Nellie giggled when Jimmy's unsteady footing caused him to fall off the pony. Miss Match patiently stood next to him, waiting for the boy to get back on his tiny feet. She then waited for him to grab onto her tail so she could lead him around the pasture.

When Jimmy went into the house for his naps, Miss Match impatiently whinnied and pawed at the ground until her playmate came back out to play with her.

The loggers and new settlers would soon be coming around looking for new horses. Tom had a fine selection, all of which were well trained. This year promised to be a profitable one.

Nellie never let on about her dreams. Most nights the same dreams haunted her again and again. She rarely got a peaceful night's rest. Each night she saw the pit of blood and the bodies laying half covered in snow. Night after night she called out Weenuk's name, and woke up trembling. As the weeks passed, she became weaker and weaker, and her eyes became more sunken. When Tom asked what was wrong, she just turned and walked away. When the water from her river, no longer gave her energy, Tom became very concerned.

Rumors swirled that the Indian villages were being hit hard by Tuberculosis. When he finally asked her if she knew anything about it, she burst into tears. She told him about her dreams and daytime visions. She talked about Manitou, and how she had been able to sit and counsel with him. She explained the tribal council's vision and why she had been chosen to live with Tom in the white man's world.

Without stopping for a breath, she told him about her kidnapping and eventual release. She discussed the fact that she was Weenuk's woman, and that she had conversations with the Spirit of the River. She spoke long and told him things she never planned on telling him or anyone else for that matter. Like the waters from a broken beaver dam, the words flowed long and strong. She finally told him about her son, and that he had been born with the spirit of Weenuk deep within him.

Tom reached out and drew her tight against him. He held her in his arms as the tears poured from her eyes. When there were no more tears, she sobbed and clung to him tightly. She spoke and sobbed until there were no more secrets. She had finally confessed her spirit.

Little Jimmy stood watching his mother cry, while his father held her in his arms. He, too, felt the sorrow and pain. His tears brought both of them back to their world.

Nellie broke free from Tom's arms and scooped Jimmy into her arms. She rocked him back and fourth in her arms, while Tom just stood and watched. Her tears were gone, but had her sorrow just begun? Had she told Tom more than she should? Would he cast her and her son away, and let the spirit of her people die?

Tom now sat upon the bed and watched the two most precious people in his world hugging and sniffling as their tears dried up. His head was spinning with the things he'd heard. He was trying to sort everything out and make sense of it all. He just sat there numbly.

Finally, he blurted out, "Nellie, it seems to me that if this Weenuk is as smart as you say he is, then he knows me pretty good. I don't care about you being his woman before. I don't care if you talk to your God. What I care about is that you have made me the proudest man in the world. Of all the people out there, he gave you to me. That tells me that he had a pretty good notion that I wouldn't care about that other stuff. All I care about is you and that boy there. If your people are going to die, there isn't anything we can do about it. We have to be real careful and make sure that we stay good and healthy."

Their lives changed in a matter of minutes. They could no longer pass each other without an affectionate glance or meaningful kiss. Their worlds were now one. All of the questions that Tom had were answered, and although some of the answers weren't quite what he would have liked, all of the pieces of the puzzle now fit. They were a family that was bound by love, understanding and respect.

Tom and Nellie finally felt comfortable asking and answering each other's questions about their pasts. Tom told her about his childhood and the drunken, abusive parents he had. He discussed the reasons why he never trusted anyone, and why he only felt comfortable with horses. For the first time in his life, he talked to someone important to him about his past and he didn't feel ashamed of it.

Weenuk no longer had time to seek out the affections of another woman. His days and nights were filled with the coughs of his weakening people. Even he had developed a deep cough that he could not shake. When he wasn't busy with his own village, other villages called for his healing powers. He spent day and night in journeys to the Underworld, chanting and trying to drive away evil spirits. Regardless of how hard he and his Spirit Helpers tried, they couldn't save the dying people. As the planting moon changed to the growing moon, the number of healing calls became even more frequent. However, it wasn't until the harvest moon arrived that his greatest challenge came.

Weenuk had barely laid his head upon his sleeping mat when his sleep was interrupted by the excited call of the Chief's woman.

"Come quick, Weenuk! The Chief is sick, and it is not like the others!"

Weenuk woke quickly and hurried to Amable du Fond's lodge. Several others were already present, and Weenuk bent over his friend. He expected to hear the coughs that kill, but instead the Chief's body was riddled with small red spots that oozed. Fever raged in the old man, and he spoke words that made little sense.

"Call my drummer, and have him bring my medicine bag. This is not like the others!" Weenuk commanded the Chief's woman with great concern.

"My friend, I am here and I will make you well." Weenuk spoke calmly to his old friend. "I shall call for Manitou to help me, for I know not of this rash or how to stop it."

Before his drummer arrived he began chanting loudly, and hovered over the Chief's body. The drummer ran through the crowd that had gathered outside the lodge, and seeing the worried look on Weenuk's face, he sat down immediately and began drumming. Weenuk began another journey to the Underworld.

Another assistant came in and filled the lodge with the smoke of sweet grass. The Chief's woman sat wide eyed and worried. The drum beat loudly and Weenuk's voice rose. His chants grew louder. His rattle added to the symphony that rose to the land of Manitou. He called the Great One desperately. The drumbeats echoed loudly throughout the bush, sending out a message to all. The great Chief Amable du Fond may soon be joining his ancestors.

Weenuk danced in a frenzy as he worked over his friend. Even those who were gravely ill themselves stood outside the Chief's lodge in silence as Weenuk's voice blended with the sounds of the drum and rattle. His feet pounded hard upon the ground, and he danced around and around. The evil spirits hovered around the old man.

Weenuk shouted, "I shall not allow you to take my friend and the Chief of our people!"

The Evil One responded angrily, "I shall do as I wish, old man, and there is nothing you can do about it. You are weak, and I am strong. If you aggravate me, I shall strike you down as well."

"My strength has been given to me by Manitou, and you are nothing but a fly on a horse's back."

"We shall soon see who is the greater spirit!"

Weenuk danced, chanted and called to Manitou, "Oh Great One, do not let the evil spirits take our Chief from us. His wisdom and bravery have been spoken of for many winters. Please let him live so that our people can continue listening to his words!"

He danced on and on. The drumbeats echoed throughout the lands of the ancestors, calling on their strength and wisdom. Still the evil spirits became stronger and began to succeed. Weenuk's chants echoed high above the land, and even the Eagle shed a tear. No matter how hard Weenuk chanted and danced, he was no match for the evil spirits that had come to stay.

The spirit of the coughing sickness had been sent to weaken

the Indians. The spirit of this new sickness—called Small Pox—was the greatest spirit the Evil One had ever devised. It came to wipe out everyone in its path. It had a hunger that could not be quenched. It traveled from village to village and infected all of the neighboring tribes, as well as the white man.

The powers of Manitou were challenged again and again. He fought hard against the Evil One every day. His people were taken from Him one at a time. The women and children were given no quarters, and the Evil One laughed when he struck them down. A war was once again being waged against the people of Manitou's land. Even He had no defense, and like the fish in a polluted pond, they died gasping for breath. The smoke from the pyres filled the skies, and even the Eagle flew to safety.

The harvest moon shone brightly and the summer's heat had finally passed. Nellie sat upon the front stoop, while Tom looked up at the stars and moon above. He asked, "What do you suppose that moon looks like up close?"

Nellie just shrugged her shoulders and continued listening to the beating of the distant drums. Both of them had worked until the sun set, cutting the hay from their field. The next day they would be loading the wagon and pitching it into the barn. Jimmy was sound asleep in his cradle and the world was still.

"Well, I guess it's time to call it a night." Tom mumbled to Nellie. He was well aware of where her thoughts were. "Are you coming?"

Without saying a word Nellie rose and walked into the cabin behind him. She still had dreams about the death that stalked her village, but she no longer panicked about it. She only felt a deep grief and sorrow. In her dreams she saw the lodges of her friends and looked upon their lifeless forms, knowing they, too, had joined their ancestors. Each night she dreamed of different lodges, not only those of her village, but those in neighboring villages. At least she was safe with her man and her son safely beside her.

"Tonight the drums are louder than on other nights," she said to Tom, then knelt down to pray to Manitou.

"Manitou, I seek your counsel, though I know you cannot come. I feel so alone, and yet my life is full. Tonight the drums of my people are loud. Please try to save some of my friends and family, especially Weenuk. Let him be safe from the claws of death that stalk our lands. Let him know that in my heart I am sad, and wish to be with him to help in whatever way I can."

That night, her dreams were very vivid. She heard many cries and wails from her village. When she stopped one of her friends to ask who had died that night, she was told the Chief had been taken. She sobbed. She wished to see Weenuk. Her wishes were granted, and she could see the old man sitting alone in his lodge. His fire burned low and it cast ugly shadows as he called out to Manitou.

"I have no more strength to save my people. My magic has no more powers, and I wish to join my friend. The evil spirits have won, and I cannot fight them any longer for I have no more to give."

"Weenuk, I have come to you. I know of your grief and I wish to comfort you." Wishna-hea spoke clearly.

"My woman, you have taken the sadness away and replaced it with great joy. I have longed to hear your words and see your smiling face. I have watched over you for as long as I could, but now my strengths are gone. I am but an old man wishing to join our ancestors. I have no more to give."

"Then let me sit beside you and hold your hands in mine."

She sat in front of him and grasped his hands. She looked into his eyes at their wonder and the years faded away. The wrinkled old man became youthful and his sorrow became joy.

They walked along the river and the birds began to sing. She turned towards him, reaching up to touch his cheek. He turned and held her closely. Their bodies pressed tightly together. He wrapped his arms around her and pressed his lips to hers. His kiss sent sparks through her body. His hands reached down and cupped her buttocks as he pulled her closer to him. She felt his member grow against her stomach and she reached up, wrapping her arms around his neck. They clung to each other and let their excitement grow.

Her knees became weak, so they laid on the ground in naked splendor. He went deep inside her, and his thrusts were strong and quick. They climbed higher and higher together, reaching for the stars.

He simply died inside her, clinging to her arms. She kissed his lips and whispered, "I shall love you forever."

The White Moose appeared beside him, and beckoned. Weenuk's spirit arose and climbed upon his back. With his youthful body once again strong, he told her, "You are the hope of our people, just as you have always been mine. Teach those who survive the ways of the white man, so they, too, can live forever and hold onto the spirit of our people. I must leave you now and join my friend on his journey to our ancestors. My spirit will remain with you."

As she knelt upon the ground, the snows began to swirl. In a blinding light of glory, he was simply no more.

She woke in silence and lay upon her bed, tears streaming down her cheeks. She felt very alone.

# Chapter 15

Now that the Chief and Weenuk both joined their ancestors, there was no one to lead the tribe or offer important wisdom. Desperate to gain control of their awful situation, the tribe appointed one of the villagers to become chief. However, a chief without a spiritual leader is like a bird without feathers. So just as with any animal of the bush, when it is frightened and has no guidance, flight is the only instinct it has left. The villagers figured that if the strong left the village, perhaps their people had a chance to survive after all.

Nellie no longer smiled and spoke very little. She knew that her vision was meant to prepare her, but the pain was simply unbearable. Tom tried humoring her whenever he could, but she only found joy in sleep, which she did whenever time allowed. She remained a good mother, and indulged Tom whenever he wished, but she had no more passion left in her.

As the winter progressed and the daylight faded, Tom started spending more time with Jimmy. It seemed the child had quite a way with horses. He even charmed the horses that came with Nellie years earlier. He often walked through the barn underneath their bellies. At first, their eyes opened wide and their ears flopped back, but now they just stood motionless and waited for him to pass.

At night Nellie sat and taught Jimmy her native tongue. Tom wasn't interested in learning her language anymore, because he no longer had any Indians to talk to since many of them died or left the area. He knew that speaking her native language helped her deal with her grief, so he enjoyed hearing her speak it with Jimmy. It gave her strength and helped her feel closer to her people.

Time became a great healer and Nellie's mood slowly began to improve. She continued to wear her small leather medicine pouch around her neck. It was her favorite possession. When alone, she held it in both hands. She never felt a need to look inside, because she knew that Weenuk's spirit would always be inside. When she held it in her hands, Weenuk's final words rang loudly in her mind, "You are the hope of our people."

Tom heard that a new depot was going to be opening between Nobosing and Wassa Lakes. He was excited because this meant that more settlers would be coming into the area, and as a result, he would get more business. In the spring he would have to travel around to pick up more horses. He thought it would be nice to take Nellie and Jimmy around with him. The trip would be good for her. Since she came to live with him, she hadn't gone any farther than his piece of land. A ride away from their home might be just what she needed, and besides, he would enjoy her company.

It was about mid-winter when Nellie decided that Jimmy should have the hair of Tom's people. She asked Tom several times if he would like Jimmy's hair short, but he simply shrugged his shoulders. He didn't want to upset Nellie, so he said nothing.

Nellie had no idea how to cut hair like the white man, so she had Tom sit on the bed while she started cutting Jimmy's hair. At first, Tom thought she was cutting his hair so short that it would never grow back; but by the time she finished, Jimmy looked like a little man. He no longer looked like a baby.

When she raised the shears to her own hair, Tom screamed in disapproval. She was so upset by his reaction that she sent him from the cabin. Some time later, when she allowed him to return, he couldn't believe his eyes. She cut off her beautiful black hair. It was now shoulder length and a little bit uneven. Although the new look surprised him, he still thought she was the most beautiful woman in the world. She took the hair scraps and wrapped a leather strip around them. He had no idea what she would do with it, but it looked kind of interesting, nonetheless.

Spring brought a rebirth of nature. The hay that had been cut last fall would be raked and piled, so they could use it for bedding this year. Their horses needed to be fattened up, but they made it through the winter without any problems. Jimmy was nearly three now, and he could ride as good as anyone. He and Miss Match were the closest of friends, and he often nagged his parents to take him on rides through the countryside.

Of all the animals, Jimmy seemed most interested in the smaller ones. Otters, squirrels and chipmunks became his favorites. His questions were endless, and Nellie enjoyed teaching him about the animals. When they were out in the bush watching the animals, Jimmy liked crawling around on his belly to get closer. At first, both of his parents thought it was the funniest thing they had ever seen, but they were amazed at how close he could get to the animals. His soothing sounds enticed the animals to come closer. When they were within a short distance from the boy, they would exchange sounds with him. Tom had never seen anything like it, and it pleased Nellie tremendously. She knew they understood each other.

When she asked Jimmy what they said, he simply replied, "They're happy we can talk."

The watchful Eagle had returned and Nellie pointed him out to Jimmy. "That is the Eagle that watches over us and tells Manitou everything."

Just as Tom had expected, more settlers came into the area, and the land took on a new look. The new settlers pushed back the bush, because their farms required large fields. The narrow trails that had once been used by the Indians were now becoming wider and marred with deep wagon tracks. The quiet wilderness was now filling with the strange noises of mooing cows and barking dogs.

The farmers had short growing seasons, but the land was fertile and crops grew quickly. When the new discovery of gold was made in the northern hills, a new swarm of men started coming to the area.

This new breed of men was different than Nellie had ever seen. Unlike the hard working loggers and farmers, these men were young and restless. Within a single summer, more than a hundred men came up the rivers. Greed was their only passion.

The sawmills ran continuously, cutting lumber for the new market that had been created. The prospectors began to settle densely into what Tom told Nellie they called towns. The townspeople were hungry, so the farmers pushed back the bush even further.

Tom's entire herd was sold off, with the exception of two of Nellie's horses, and of course, Miss Match. This meant that he had to go off and bring in new stock. The closest place he could go to was Mattawa, and Nellie had never seen that town before. With all the new folks in the area, he didn't feel comfortable leaving her and Jimmy behind, so he packed up his family and boarded up the cabin. He didn't want to take any chances that someone would bother their things while they were away. The weather promised to be good, and they were all excited about their trip. Nellie couldn't wait to see the new town.

Before they left, Tom handed her a package that he bought for her more than three years earlier. When she opened it, she couldn't believe her eyes. Inside the box, was the most beautiful dress she had ever seen in her life. Excited, she ran inside and put it on.

When she was ready, they all headed out on horseback to Mattawa. They decided to take their time, because they didn't want to tire out Miss Match, whose legs were much shorter than the other horses. Besides, it was Jimmy's first long ride and they didn't want to tire him out either. Their saddlebags were packed with everything they needed for their trip, and they were hoping for an eventful journey.

Tom hadn't made this trip in more than five years. The loggers and settlers had changed the trail noticeably. Wagon tracks wound through the bush like ribbons, and the loggers made the trail wide enough for two wagons. There also seemed to be far less wildlife in the area.

Nellie traveled this same trail with her people for as long as she could remember. It was the main trail to Allumette Island, the summer home for her people. She, too, was amazed at how much the trail had changed. Areas that were once low lying and normally boggy were now what Tom called "corduroy roads." The loggers cut down trees and laid the logs crosswise, creating a nearly solid road of rounded logs. At first, the horses balked at their uneven footing, but soon they grew accustomed to the logs.

The trail, for the most part, followed the river. Along the way, they passed several groups of young and eager riders. These groups usually had two or three riders on horseback, leading packhorses that were heavily burdened. It occurred to Tom that they were probably heading to the gold fields. These men had far fewer supplies and provisions than the settlers, and they didn't appear to be used to hard work like the loggers. They all rode hard and their horses were typically in poor shape. Both Tom and Nellie doubted that either the riders or their horses would last through the first winter. Most of them were rude and arrogant. Their comments and stares were usually less than friendly, and they usually pointed towards Nellie. Tom was glad that he wore his gun belt in full view. His rifle was considerably more accurate, but the pistol appeared to be far more threatening.

Half way through the ride, Jimmy started complaining, so they decided to take a rest. Since Nellie's knowledge of the river was infinitely better than Tom's, she led the way to a secluded spot on the riverbank, where she knew the fish would be plentiful.

The massive pines afforded shade and soft bedding, and the

breeze coming off the river whispered through their bows, soon lulling Jimmy fast to sleep. Tom cut himself a young sapling and prepared to do some fishing, but Nellie had a different idea on how they could spend this time together. As soon as Tom sat down at the riverbank, Nellie slipped the dress over her head and carefully laid it on the ground. She had no intentions of waiting until they got home before showing Tom her appreciation for her new dress.

They ended up spending the rest of the day and night in that very spot. The fish were large and Tom caught enough fish to fill their bellies twice. While Tom fished, Nellie and Jimmy enjoyed the comforts of the river.

It had been a long time since Nellie swam in a river. The small creek that wound through their property was hardly deep enough to swim in even though there were a few wide pools. She waited until Tom finished fishing so he could watch Jimmy, while she swam out into the river's depths. It felt strange not having her long hair trailing behind her, but she didn't let that bother her wonderful, relaxing swim.

Tom and Jimmy stayed close to the shore, while she swam beneath the surface. Her body twisted and glided through the water. During her swim she couldn't help thinking about the last time she swam in a river's depths. It had been the day before she was brought to Tom, when she spoke to the Spirit of the River. All rivers have their own spirits, and she tried beckoning the spirit of this river. No matter how hard she tried, however, she could not summon the spirit, so she continued her swim, enjoying the coolness of the water and the company of the fishes.

Nellie had forgotten how good it felt to camp along the river and lead an expedition along the riverbank. She found all kinds of things left behind by her people. Tom was amazed at her astute exploration abilities. Most of the items would have been easily passed over by a white man.

With each new find, she told a story of the person who had left it behind. As Tom watched and listened to her, he thought about how much she had given up when she came to live with him. He thought about how shallow his life was before, and how much fuller it had become since her arrival.

They spent the rest of the day exploring and enjoying the area. Tom couldn't remember the last time he enjoyed himself that much. When night came, Jimmy quickly fell asleep. Tom and Nellie sat beside the river's edge, watching the full moon and the stars twinkling above. The rippling of the water and the sounds of nighttime were intoxicating.

"What was this country like before we came here?" he asked quietly.

"You mean before the white man came into our lands?" she questioned earnestly.

"Just like it was before people lived and only animals and Manitou walked the lands." Tom's questions continued. "How old do you think He is?"

Nellie was pleased that Tom asked about Him. He rarely seemed interested in learning anything about Manitou.

"He is as old as the mountains and this river. When He walked this land, He knew of the greatness that stretched out before Him. He taught the birds to fly and the fish to swim. It is said that he is the father of Mother Earth and everything that lived on the land." They sat together in tranquility.

Nellie pointed to the brightest star in the sky and said, "The star that is brighter than the others is the spirit of Weenuk. All other stars are the spirits of my people that have joined our ancestors. Grandmother Moon is the eye of Manitou, for He watches over all the lands. Someday my spirit will shine from above, and you will talk to me, and then you will understand the words of the twinkling."

Tom sat speechless looking deep at the vastness of the universe, and was mesmerized by its beauty. Before Nellie came into this life, he never even took notice of the stars. He was beginning to understand the beauty and delicate balance of the universe, and Nellie understood his understanding.

It had been a long time since Nellie slept under the stars,

and between her love for her man, and the stars above, they slept very little.

In the morning, Tom awoke before Nellie and went immediately to the river, where he tossed his line out. Nellie stirred when she heard Tom whooping and hollering down by the water's edge. He hollered for her to join him, and when she reached the river, Tom was standing waist deep in water and his long, flexible pole was bent nearly in half. She ran to the bank and laughed as Tom nearly fell in. Did Tom have the fish, or did the fish have Tom?

By the time the fish tired out, Tom managed to stumble and fall into the water three times. He was determined not to lose this beauty. The fish was almost as long as his arm and fatter than his thigh. They spent a good part of the morning drying out Tom's clothes and eating the huge fish. The sun was almost directly above their camp, when they decided to finally head out again.

Tom barely knew the horse trader they were going to visit. All he knew was that the man's ethics were less than admirable. The last time he saw him, Tom was new to the area and didn't really know anyone. At that time, the trader, Fred Johnson, impressed Tom as being a skinflint that would burn you if you gave him half a chance. Tom had come out of their trade slightly ahead, but it had taken nearly a full day to settle the deal. If he remembered correctly, Fred was not too happy when they parted.

The town was built up quite a bit since Tom was last there. He was glad that Fred's place was on the outskirts of town, so he didn't have to ride into town to ask for directions.

Fred owned quite a property. Tom counted thirty or so horses in the pasture as they were riding in. The barns were in a state of disrepair, but the house was impeccable. The only houses Nellie had ever seen were small cabins, and compared to them, this house was a mansion. It had two stories with a long porch that ran across the front and wrapped around the side of the building. It was painted white and had spindle railings around the porch.

"Bonjour friend, what can I do for you?" bellowed a loud voice from the first barn, as they approached.

Before Tom could answer, a fat man with beady eyes walked up to them and started hollering to someone inside the barn, "Get out here squaw, and take care of these fine folks' horses!" He glanced at Tom quickly, then to Nellie. His sneer made a statement that was louder than words.

Before Tom could answer his original question, he added, "Well, seeing you don't have any extra horses, you sure aren't looking to trade anything, except maybe this here squaw!" His eyes lit up as he focused on Nellie's thin waist. "A fine looker, too."

"You haven't changed a bit, you old bastard, have you?" Tom snapped sarcastically.

"I know you, friend?" Fred questioned.

"First of all, we aren't friends, and second of all, you happen to be talking about my woman, so you better put your damned eyes back into their sockets." Tom's voice was both direct and commanding.

"Sorry friend, but we don't get to see many young, pretty squaws around these parts, unless they work at the hotel." Fred paused then continued, "No offense intended." Then he finally pried his eyes from Nellie's slender body.

"Say, haven't I seen you before? Aren't you that trader that moved up river some years back?"

"Sure am, and I've come to see what you have for horse meat here."

"We have the finest horse flesh within fifty miles!" He spoke proudly while checking out Tom and Nellie's horses closely.

Tom finally dismounted and signaled Nellie and Jimmy to do the same.

A heavyset squaw came out from the barn, and Nellie's eyes lit up. She hadn't expected to see a squaw with the white man.

The squaw's face was drawn and one of her eyes was badly blackened. She looked up at Nellie and quickly lowered her eyes, obviously ashamed of being there.

Nellie made no comment, but knew instantly that she was

Albnoki. Although the two tribes had never been considered friendly, they never had any bad blood between them either.

The woman took the reins from Tom and Jimmy, and when Nellie started to follow her with her horse, Tom held his hand out low and flat, signaling her to hold her ground, while he stood squarely in front of Fred.

"Dear, you want to take this fine woman's horse, too?" Fred spoke loudly to the squaw with a sarcastic sneer. His eyes fixed on the two horses.

"You have some fine looking horses there. Are you looking to trade?"

"Nope. These horses are riding back with me. I just came to see what you have, and maybe I can take a couple of horses off your hands."

"Well, seeing that you don't have anything to trade, then you must have some cash, right friend? How much do you have with you?" His beady eyes got even smaller.

"Well, I'm not saying I do or saying I don't. All I'm saying is that I haven't seen anything here that would be much better than supper meat." The negotiations were beginning.

Nellie took Jimmy by the hand and led her horse in the direction of the other squaw. It would be a long afternoon.

Nellie was eager to talk to the other woman and find out if she knew where her people went. The other woman didn't speak the same language so they resorted to signing, which was the universal language of all tribes. It was slow and agonizing, but the meanings were eventually understood.

Jimmy got bored quickly. He wanted to see everything he could see and touch everything he wasn't supposed to touch. Nellie did her best to contain his energy and excitement.

Nellie learned that many tribes traveled down the river to escape the evil spirits, and rumor had it, they traveled in the direction of the rising sun. The squaw knew no other information, and she was reluctant to speak anymore to Nellie. Their conversation ended when the squaw started to cough violently and told Nellie to take her son and leave immediately.

By the time Tom concluded his business, he was the proud owner of two teams and two saddle horses. He intended on buying more, but apparently the price of horseflesh had risen drastically. If he had known that before, he would have charged much more for the horses he had already sold.

Nellie was anxious to see what a town looked like, and since it was late afternoon, they decided to ride into town. The town consisted of three wide streets with buildings on both sides. All of the buildings were tall enough to accommodate two floors. Some of the buildings were made of stone and were enormous compared to even Fred's house. They rode up one street and down the next checking out each and every building.

The main street had wooden paths in front of the buildings. Tom told Nellie and Jimmy that these wooden paths were created, so that people didn't have to walk in the mud when it rained or the snow melted.

Excitedly, they tied up their horses and began their exploration. The smell of fresh cooked food came from the hotel's kitchen, so they decided to head there first. When they entered the hotel, they took a table close to the door and ordered steak, beans and apple pie. Nellie never tasted anything as good as the apple pie before, and it didn't take long to convince her to order seconds. The hotel was quite busy. Nellie and Jimmy were fascinated by the people and the clothes they wore. Surprisingly, she didn't see any other Indian women at the hotel.

Next, they headed to the general store, which turned out to be Nellie's favorite place in town. She was amazed by the assortment of goods and supplies, and she had to examine almost every single item on the shelves. At first it was fun, but then Tom became impatient when she kept asking so many questions. She was particularly interested in the bolts of material. Before they left, she had enough material to make a brand new dress. She finished up her shopping spree with some needles and thread. Tom ended up buying candy sticks for all of them.

After everything was explored, they rode out of town and found a secluded place along the river to spend the night.

# Chapter 16

They started out shortly after daybreak. Nellie led the two saddle horses and Tom led the others. Jimmy's pony didn't like being last, so she ran in front with Nellie and the larger horses. Before too long, her legs grew tired and she found herself at the end of the procession once again. Both Nellie and Tom had their hands full. The new horses they acquired were one step from being wild, and they didn't like being led one bit. It wasn't until midday when they finally settled down, and the ride became more pleasant for everyone.

They decided to take a midday rest along the river. The horses were tired, so they let them roam in the grassy meadow that lined the riverbank, while Tom fished for dinner. Jimmy wanted his mother's attention, so as soon as the fire was made, the pair walked leisurely through the long grass.

Nellie pointed to the Eagle, which was no more than a dot in the sky. She told him that the Eagle has been her friend since she was a child. She then reached down and picked up her son, hugging him tenderly.

"When you grow up to be big and strong, he will watch over you, just like he watches over me."

"Why does he do that?"

"Because you are a lot more special than you will ever know. Manitou has sent the Eagle to watch over us and protects us."

"Does that mean that you are special too, Ma?"

"I guess so. I'm special so I can watch over you."

Jimmy reached up and kissed his mother on the cheek. "I like being special with you, Ma. Is Pa special, too?"

"Yes. We are all special, and Manitou says so."

After they finished their meal, Jimmy slept soundly on the grass, while Nellie calmed the horses. Tom went back to the river to catch one more fish before they left. The rest of the day went slowly, and it was nearly dark before they reached the comforts of their cabin.

It had taken a while, but Weenuk's spirit had finally finished its metamorphosis. He now sat at the fire pit of Manitou. He no longer had any earthly duties. Instead, he sat around the fire with his ancestors and talked about old times. It was nice to see the others, especially his father, who he hadn't spoken to in more than forty years.

Laughter was one thing that surprised Weenuk. When he walked on Earth as a man, he didn't have much time for laughter. Now with Manitou and the others, he laughed often.

When they reached their cabin, Nellie put Jimmy to bed, while Tom bedded the horses. It had been a long day and everyone was exhausted. Nellie put her head on the pillow, not bothering to light a lantern. In the darkness, she bumped her hand on something solid. As soon as her hand wrapped around the object, she knew exactly what it was—it was the doll she had left behind.

The doll's body was made from a branch, which had been wrapped with a series of deer hide strips. The doll was dressed in a buckskin dress decorated with beads. As long as she could remember, this doll was her most cherished possession.

She cradled it in her arms just as she had with Jimmy, and tears streamed down her cheeks. There was only one possible explanation. Weenuk had returned. He knew how much the doll meant to her. He had watched as she kissed her doll one last time, before she left. She held the doll to her chest and rocked slowly with her eyes closed.

Her mind swam with memories that she had all but forgotten. The dress on the doll had to be replaced when the first one wore out. She once took the doll swimming with her, but ended up spending hours rubbing bear fat into the hide to soften it back up. She remembered everything vividly. Her mother had pleaded with her to leave it behind when she became Weenuk's woman, but she blatantly refused.

When Tom walked in the door, she laid her head down on the pillow. She said nothing to him. Instead, she held her doll against her shoulder and fell fast asleep. She planned to tell Tom about the doll in the morning.

Her dream began nearly as soon as her eyes closed. She sat beside the fire pit in Weenuk's lodge and he sat directly across from her. His body was strong and youthful, and his wrinkles were gone. His silver hair was now the color of midnight. His eyes sparkled like the flickering flames of the fire, and their words passed as thoughts.

"It is good to see you again!" Weenuk started the conversation.

"I missed you. But you appear much younger than I remember you."

"I appear as I remember me, not the old man your eyes were accustomed to."

"Tell me of the lands of our ancestors. Is it as I have seen when we sat in council with Manitou?"

"No, it is filled with conversations with our ancestors and friends. They are all young and strong, and we talk long." His voice was soft and soothing.

"What do you talk about? How do you feel?"

"We talk about the same things we spoke of when we walked, but we speak fully, and our thoughts are much kinder."

"Do you like it?"

"It is different, but the difference is good. We are saddened by the end of our ways, but there is no more pain and sorrow."

"What have you learned since you got there?" Wishna-hea asked inquisitively.

"I have learned the answers to all questions, but sometimes they shouldn't be asked."

"What does my future hold for me, and what lies ahead for our son?"

"Those are questions that should not be asked, for the future is one that must be discovered. Behind every tree lies another tree that is different, yet the same. Tomorrow holds good for those who seek goodness. Look for good things and don't worry about tomorrow. All things will come."

"Will our son live to be a wise old man?"

"Our son was born with wisdom and will learn its meaning in time."

Nellie's tone changed. "Why have our people died, and why must our ways die with them?"

"We lived as our ancestors have since Manitou walked as man, and we must give up our lands so others may live. One day our people will return and once again walk our lands. For now, we must allow the others to come, and we shall learn from their wisdom."

"How will we know if their wisdom is good and their ways are just?"

"Time is like the waters of a river. It changes directions many times. Eventually it finds its way. No direction is right or wrong, only different."

"What wisdom can you give me that will make my life better?"

"The feelings for your white man are good, and he feels the same about you. I am pleased with my choice of men. His heart is true and kind. Continue learning his ways. His heart is good for you and our child."

"Does that mean that he does not love our son?"

"His love for our son is strong and good, but a time will come when he must choose. His heart will choose you over all of the Mother Earth. His heart is true and he feels strong."

Their conversations continued for most of the night, and many questions were asked and answered. Weenuk assured her that they would share many more dreams together.

Nellie woke to the sound of the rooster calling, totally refreshed and filled with joy. She couldn't wait to tell Tom about her dream and show him what Weenuk had left her. However, he was so tired from last night's work that she didn't want to disturb his much needed sleep. So she decided to wait for him to wake naturally.

The bird's song echoed as Nellie opened the door and went outside. Within a few moments, she had smoke curling up from the fire pit, and she clung fiercely to her doll. Today she did not pray to Mother Earth, but instead prayed to Manitou to thank him for allowing Weenuk to be her spirit guide.

She prepared the morning soup and went to the fence to watch the horses in the pasture. The new horses were already accustomed to the others. They learned quickly on the long ride from Mattawa. Today they would begin their lessons, and she was very excited about teaching them.

She went into the barn, came out with two brushes and entered the pasture. Her horse immediately began walking towards her, followed closely by the rest of the herd. She enjoyed watching her horse and relished the time they spent together.

She needed something to keep her occupied and this would serve well. She exploded with excitement and wanted to wake up both Tom and Jimmy so she could tell them her wonderful news. But they really needed their sleep, so she waited patiently.

She tucked her doll into the front of her dress and began brushing her horse. Tom often asked her what her horse's name was, and she always answered the same thing—he didn't have a name. The truth was she couldn't put a name on anything she did not intend to enjoy for the rest of her life. Part of horse trading involved giving up horses, and she couldn't bear the thought of losing a horse that she had named.

She continued brushing her horse until his entire body glistened. She used one hand to brush and the other to smooth. Since the horses' hierarchy had to be maintained, she then brushed out Tom's horse, followed by Miss Match. She eventually worked her way through the entire herd.

She didn't stop brushing the horses until she heard movement from inside the cabin. Jimmy was always the first to awake, and Nellie secretly enjoyed having Tom wake to Jimmy's quiet footsteps.

As soon as the door opened in front of her, she held the doll out proudly.

"Look! My doll!" she exclaimed. "My doll has been returned to me."

"What do you mean, it's been returned to you? Do you mean you found it someplace?"

"No. It's a gift from Weenuk!"

"But I thought you told me he's been dead for more than half a year now?" Tom was dumfounded.

"Yes, but he gave me the doll, and I talked to him in my dream."

"Well, if you were talking to him in your dream, how did you get the doll?"

"It was just there on my pillow."

"Do you mean he sent someone here during the night to put it there?"

"No! No one came. The doll just appeared on my pillow."

"How do you suppose it got here?" Tom questioned further.

"Weenuk is a powerful man. His spirit brought the doll."

"So does that mean, we have his ghost in the cabin now?" Tom questioned, his eyebrows raised.

"His spirit protects me."

"So can his spirit see us any time he wants?" His questions now were becoming pointed.

"Yes, it sees us all the time."

After they finished the morning meal, Nellie was the first into the pasture with the horses. Tom held Jimmy in his arms, while they both watched her work her wonders with the wild horses.

By now the horses were accustomed to her presence. Nellie placed her hand on the first horse's head and gently pulled it towards her. Her words flowed softly. The horse eased his head in the right direction. His ears perked up and pointed towards her. A soft breeze came from her lips and the horse's eyes locked on her.

She said, "I am your friend, and I shall not harm you!"

Within a short time, she had the horse chest high in the river's water and she sat calmly upon his back. The horse's ears lay flat against his head and his nostrils flared. He avoided bucking because he didn't want to lose his footing on the uneven river bottom.

Nellie slipped a bridle over his nose and began gently easing him forward. It didn't take long before he understood her command and complied. Within an hour she had the horse understanding and following her basic commands. This amazed Tom because it sometimes took him a week or more to teach horses the same thing it took her less than an hour to teach. She definitely understood the horses much better than he did.

By the end of the day, all of the horses were accustomed to Nellie's commands. Although she only rode them in the water that day, they would all be comfortable riding with her anywhere in two days time.

After Nellie trained the horses, Tom had to spend time getting comfortable with each of the horses, too. There were substantial differences between their riding styles, so the horses had to become accustomed to both styles. After they accepted Tom, he began training them with full harnesses and eventually with the wagons. After several weeks of constant training, the horses became calm enough to work as a team.

While Tom focused his attention on the horses, Nellie continued teaching Jimmy the ways of her people. She now focused her lessons on the prayers that were as old as Mother Earth herself. Once he became familiar with the prayers, she wanted to teach him about the spirits. She taught the lessons the same way she'd learned them. All of the lessons were told in story form, and Jimmy listened with keen interest. He liked all of the stories, especially the ones about how his mother received her strength and courage from the Spirit of the River, how she received her faith from Manitou, and how Weenuk rescued her from her captors.

Her stories went on to explain the importance of honest and trust. He learned that courage and bravery came from an intense knowledge of the spirits that watched over him. She spoke often of different animals of the bush, and how each served a different and vital roll in the ways of nature. Jimmy knew the names of most of the animals and when she referred to the ones he liked, his eyes lit up.

Jimmy's lessons were repeated until he remembered each story completely. Tom and Nellie were delighted when he chimed in during their stories to tell them what would happen next. He was learning his lessons quickly. When Nellie asked him if he would like to meet some of the spirits, Jimmy was delighted. However, Tom was more than a little reluctant. Even though he understood parts of her spirituality, he did not like the idea of meeting these spirits, or ghosts as he called them, face to face.

Despite Tom's reluctance to take the lessons to the next level, Nellie began the first spirit ceremony by lighting the fire. She showed Tom how to beat the spirit drum, as she held smoldering sweet grass over her head. Jimmy was quite excited about the whole thing. He liked listening to his father play the drums and his mother sing out loudly. Her voice carried high into the wind, to the land of Manitou. Her voice summoned the elders. It had been a long time since she spoke to them, but soon she was able to catch their attention.

Tom had no idea of what to expect, but he eagerly awaited each step of the process. He watched and listened to the droning sounds that came from deep inside Nellie. The crisp sound seemed to waver between two tones that were much higher than her normal speech. He watched her closely. The smoke began to settle and spread like a cloud over them. Soon both Nellie and Jimmy faded from Tom's view as the cloud's density increased.

Through the smoke he thought he saw the image of several

men standing together, but then again, he wasn't sure. The images were undefined and faded in and out. He was startled when he felt a strong hand upon his shoulder, and he dared not look at it. The pressure from the hand continued its firm grip. Frightened that the hand belonged to a ghost and not a human, he stared straight ahead. Slowly, he became aware of the warmth that generated from the hand. His fear was diminishing, but he still couldn't bring himself to look at the hand. He remained unable to move for what seemed like ages. The dense smoke began swirling around him.

He wished he had the strength to ask questions, but he was afraid to hear the answers, so he sat in silence. His other senses began to intensify. The sweet-smelling smoke glowed in the fire's reflection. He felt no wind, but he heard it blowing in the distance. He strained to hear other sounds, but the only thing he could hear was the loud thumping of his heart.

He mustered enough courage to mutter, "Who are you?"

"I am your friend and you have pleased me." The words echoed in his mind.

"Who are you?" he repeated.

"Don't ask me foolish questions. You know who I am. You have felt my presence many times, but have never accepted it. I mean you no harm. Your woman has brought you to our home so that you will know me, and this pleases me."

Tom's courage was challenged, and he forced himself to turn around and look for the source of the voice. Slowly, he looked behind him, but he couldn't see anything. However, he still felt a hand on his shoulder.

"Are you Weenuk?" Tom asked sheepishly.

No words were spoken, but he knew the answer. Slowly the smoke dissipated, and once again Nellie and Jimmy were looking at him. Nellie's eyes sparkled as they locked with Tom's eyes. It took a moment to break their connection, but when he did, he instinctively looked at Jimmy. The young boy's eyes were large and he was smiling happily, but Tom could see right through him. He looked like a ghost!

Was he imagining things or was this real? All kinds of thoughts filled his mind. He was scared, but he was also curious about what was happening to his family.

He thought to himself, "Did Nellie plan this lesson for Jimmy or for me?"

# Chapter 17

Nellie's occasional cough was now becoming more persistent, and on occasions, she had to stop to catch her breath. Tom expressed his concerns, but she trivialized it, saying that it would go away in a day or two.

Since business was so good, Tom continued acquiring new horses. He usually didn't buy wild horses this late in the year, but he couldn't resist the great prices. Nellie continued training the horses to become riders, then she handed them over to Tom so he could finish their education.

Horses working in a team had to learn how to be at ease with one another, so their stalls were always adjacent to each other. The wall that divided the stalls was made of stacked logs. The spaces between these heavy logs allowed the horses an opportunity to communicate freely, but they also kept the horses from nipping at each other.

As a rule, before Tom hooked a team together, he liked to put the horses to pasture so they could rip, kick or do anything they wanted to in order to get rid of their raw energy. He didn't believe in rushing this part of the process.

"As long as you give them a chance to get rid of their fire, you won't get burned."

Tom surprised Nellie during the summer by trading one of his horses for a brand new cook stove. Although it took time for her to get used to the oven, she soon learned how to make delicious biscuits and bread. So now each morning, Tom and

Jimmy woke up to the smell of fresh baked bread and either soup or beans.

Before long, both Jimmy and Tom caught Nellie's cough. They often joked about who caught the cough from whom, but since it was only slight, they didn't really get overly concerned about it.

Their library now consisted of seven books, and both Tom and Nellie took turns reading to Jimmy. The truth was, both of them enjoyed reading a great deal and they often joked about whose turn it was to read to Jimmy.

Jimmy's fourth birthday was coming soon, and Nellie wondered where the time had gone. Since he was born, so many things had happened. It had been nearly two years since she began teaching him about his native ways and spirituality. He had grown so quickly. He even learned how to tease the ancestors during spirit meetings.

Nellie normally called for a meeting with the ancestors when the moon was full, but since their coughs were becoming more persistent, she decided to call a meeting when the moon was only half full.

The aroma of sweet grass filled the air, and the smoke swirled around the cabin. The flames from the small fire flared and the entire room glowed. The ancestors were proud of Nellie's powers and often enjoyed watching her work.

"We welcome you and wish to seek counsel." Nellie petitioned.

"We are pleased to be with you."

The smoke settled and several of the ancestors were present. Nellie was surprised that Weenuk chose not to sit in, and this made her feel a bit uncomfortable

"Why is Weenuk not present at the council? Is something wrong?"

There was a pause, and Nellie felt unsettled. Tom noticed her reaction and wondered why she was so upset. During their meetings ancestors came and left, the faces were always changing.

Chief du Fond spoke clearly, "He went on a journey with an old friend and did not anticipate your request. But I am sure he is fine and will know of our meeting."

The Chief enjoyed seeing Jimmy. Before each meeting he thought up a different name to call Jimmy. It was a game they played when meetings got boring. The best part of the game was that no one else could hear his words passing.

Jimmy's eyes always lit up when he saw that his friend was there. A simple nod was the customary acknowledgment, but Jimmy never liked that rule. He always wanted to run over and wrap his arms around the Chief's neck, but knew that he couldn't.

They all passed around the friendship pipe in acknowledgment and thanks to the others.

"It is good that we sit and smoke the pipe, and that you have called us to join you. We also know why you wish our counsel. But first, we should be social, for it is the beginning of the season of growing."

Nellie knew this was a stalling tactic, but she wasn't sure why they would stall. She just remained silent and skeptical of their actions. Tom was watching Nellie more than the others, and he knew something was wrong. The silent messages seemed to be going from the Chief to both Nellie and Jimmy. He couldn't hear what they were saying, but he saw that the conversations between Nellie and Jimmy were different.

"Son of Tadpole." Chief du Fond's thoughts playfully reached out to Jimmy.

"Chief Wrinkles." Jimmy blurted out.

The Chief was caught totally off guard, and he burst into laughter.

"You got me there!"

The Chief was about to tell Jimmy that his mother's childhood name was Tadpole, but he never got the chance.

"Why do you call me Son of Tadpole? Because I squirm a lot?"

"No, Jimmy. That is what they called me when I was small like you!" Nellie answered.

Now, everyone laughed.

The Chief's thoughts passed silently. "My tadpole has grown, and I wish to be allowed to play with your son before he must sleep."

"Why must he sleep?"

"Because it is best for him to sleep."

"Did my Ma squirm a lot, too?" Jimmy asked the Chief.

Everyone laughed again, and Jimmy fell asleep listening to their laughter.

"It has been more than two winters since most of us came here. We have learned much since we first arrived. Even Weenuk, whose wisdom was far greater than mine, has learned a great deal." The Chief said sternly.

"What is this wisdom telling you right now?" Nellie didn't like the tone of this council at all, and her words became sharp.

"We have learned that there is a time for all things. Just as there is a time for planting and harvesting, there is a time to leave the lands that we love and respect."

Nellie tried to speak, but she choked up. She paused for a moment to regain her composure. "Are you saying that it is my time to leave this land?"

"We are saying that there is a time for all things to pass."

"What are you saying?" Tom could no longer contain himself and his voice rose in anger.

With his raised voice, the images of the elders began to fade.

"Please . . . Come back!" Nellie pleaded in earnest.

# Chapter 18

"We wish not to anger, only enlighten." Chief replied regretfully.

"Please tell me which of us will be joining you? Please?" Nellie pleaded.

The Chief did not reply. He simply looked upon them all.

"Is this what has killed my people?" Without waiting for a reply, both Nellie and Tom knew the answer.

They reached out to each other and grasped their hands together. Even though Tom was an outsider and was forbidden to talk during council meetings, he blurted out, "Why? You told her that she was to be spared, and that she and Jimmy were the hope of your people. Take me and only me. Let them live. I beg you!"

"It is not our wish to watch you plead for the lives of your family. You were chosen to show Wishna-hea love and understanding. Your love for family is perhaps even greater than ours. It is believed that in your previous life you were one of us. Because of this, we will allow you to speak. But speak wisely, for you are being judged."

Tom wasn't sure if he should stand or remain seated, so he instinctively stood. Nellie put her hand on his shoulder, signaling that he should remain seated and that she was very proud of him.

"Chief, it's not that I'm ungrateful or anything like that. But you promised that she and the boy would both live a long time. Heck, it hasn't even been two years since you said that! You just can't take them now!"

"We have kept our word. She was and is the hope of our people. When there seemed to be no hope for any of us, she was there."

Before Tom could interrupt the Chief continued, "It took all of our powers to shield her from harm. She proved her bravery time and again. Manitou told us of her greatness, and that only love could shield her. Manitou has told us that you have loved her from the instant you saw her, and that you have always treated her as a friend. You have shared your ways with her and have worked hard to understand our ways. You have known of this coughing death since you first heard her cough, yet you remained in her bed. You raised the child you knew had the spirit of Weenuk, and yet you didn't ask why. Your love is far greater than ours."

"I just love her with all my heart, Sir, that's all. Hell, I love Jimmy because he's my son, our son. I wouldn't give a thousand horses for one of his hairs or hers for that matter." Tom whispered softly.

"We can't change what is unchangeable. But we cannot let your words go unheeded. You did not speak once of yourself, only of your love." A long pause ensued.

Nellie squeezed Tom's hands in hers and their eyes met. She looked over at Jimmy asleep on the floor and gently picked him up. She held him close to her chest, and Tom hugged them both, while they waited for the Chief to make his decision.

"It is true that we cannot change what is unchangeable, but we can postpone . . ."

Neither Nellie nor Tom heard him finish. They squeezed each other tightly, and sighed in relief.

"How long can you postpone this for?" They asked in unison.

"Life is for living. Don't think of how long; only think of how much."

"Is there anything we can do to help?" Tom asked.

"Wishna-hea, it has been more than two years since you last swam in your river. You must go back and gain strength from the Spirit of the River." Weenuk said from behind the others.

Startled, Nellie jumped and blurted, "Why didn't you make your presence known?"

"It was time for your man to speak, and if I was there, he would not have spoken." Weenuk's wisdom was displayed, once again.

The smoke began rising into the wind, signaling the end of their session. Before they knew it, the ancestors disappeared entirely. Both Nellie and Tom were left gazing into the burning embers of the fire.

Nellie's trance wore off first and she reached over to Tom, shaking his shoulder softly, "Tom, we must go now."

"You mean, we have to go today?"

"Yes. We're going to the river as soon as we get the horses fed and ready. Get up and get them started. I'm going to warm the soup and I'll be right out. I'll let Jimmy sleep until we're ready to go."

"Well, if this is the way it has to be, then I guess there isn't anything else we can do about it. Just think what it would have been like if we didn't have those ancestors on our side."

It was late morning before they headed out to the river. During their ride, Nellie and Tom's thoughts focused on their memories. Nellie thought about her people who no longer existed. She thought about their celebrations and their games. Each of her friends faded in and out of her thoughts. She remembered most of them as happy and smiling people.

She thought about the dresses Tom bought her, and the first time she became his woman. She smiled when she remembered watching him shoe a horse for the first time, and when he began teaching her to read from his precious books.

Meanwhile, Tom had memories of his own. He remembered wetting his pants just before Weenuk sprung Nellie on him, and how embarrassed he was when he first saw how beautiful she was. He thought about how excited she was to learn how to use the plow and read. He remembered her smiling face after she gave birth to Jimmy. But most of all, he thought about their times of passion and love.

The ride was nearly half over when they snapped out of their trances and looked into each other's eyes. They smiled and realized that they really did have a lot to be grateful for. Tom put his arm around Nellie's shoulder and drew her tight against him.

The birds' songs filled the air, as they rode through the wide trails that led through the bush. The trees had not yet blossomed, but the sun's rays were strong. Nellie was surprised at how quickly the bush changed. The new growth was already growing where the loggers cut down old trees. There was beauty even among man's destruction. She took the reins, because she was coming home.

"How much farther do we have to ride?" Jimmy asked his mother.

"It won't be long. We'll be there soon." Nellie answered as she reached around behind her and lifted Jimmy up to sit on her lap.

"Can I drive, Ma?"

"Sure," she replied as she handed him the reins. "You can drive for a while."

Jimmy was so excited! They were not only going to see where his mother lived, but they were going to stay there for a few days. And to top it all off, they were sleeping outdoors. This was a whole new adventure. The wagon had been loaded with some supplies, and after they reached their destination, his mother told him there would be a surprise. He just couldn't wait.

Nellie caught the scent of her river at the same time as the horses. They picked up their pace, and Nellie took over the reins. She clucked and spoke loudly, "Giddy yup!"

The sound of the wagon, with all of its squeaks and rattles rambled on. The animals scattered because it had been a long time since they heard that sound. Ever since the loggers found the deserted village with half-eaten Indian carcasses, they swore it was haunted, and everyone gave the area wide birth. The land had become sacred, for without being properly attended, their spirits became "Earth locked" and could not join their ancestors.

Only those with special powers had been allowed to leave. Everyone waited for her return.

Tom felt their presence, and a chill ran up his spine. He knew where they were going, but he had no idea of what to expect. He heard all of the rumors and stories about the ghosts that haunted the area, and like most white men, he feared ghosts. Even though Nellie was with him and he had seen the spirits in council, he was still afraid. The closer they came to the river, the stronger the feeling became. Tom was nearly ready to wet his pants, when Nellie slowly reached behind him and pinched his side.

He jumped off the seat, and Nellie and Jimmy laughed at his reaction.

"Damn it, woman! You nearly scared me to death. That's not funny!"

Now they both laughed even harder. "Pa is a scaredy-cat." Jimmy mocked his father's reactions, as he jumped up as high as he could.

Both Tom and Nellie now laughed together, but it still didn't relieve his uneasiness. He was entering a world that he knew little about.

The wagon carried them past the first sight of water, and the air seemed cooler. The giant pines towered above, and the wind whispered through them. At first, Tom thought he heard voices, but then he realized it was only the wind. Nellie let go of the reins, because the horses were now home, too. Even though they had never been there, instinctively they knew the way.

Each of them watched the bush closely, looking for any sign of movement. Tom lifted his rifle, but then thought about how useless it was, and propped it against the seat. Nellie understood his fear, because she had fears of her own. Would the spirits welcome her now that she brought a white man with her? Would they listen to the words of Manitou? Tom had reasons to be afraid, and she was afraid for him.

The river and its babbling current grew louder. Nellie always knew that she would return some day, and her heart pumped faster, as she approached her beloved river.

A shiver came over Tom, and he looked over at Jimmy sitting on his mother's lap. The young boy rubbed his arms to warm himself, and Nellie instinctively wrapped her arms around him to add further warmth, and also to protect him. Unconsciously, Nellie also squeezed the leather sack that hung from her neck. If ever she needed the powers from her medicine sack, then this was the time. She slowly slid the strap over her head, and both Jimmy and Tom watched her intently.

Her eyes met theirs and then looked back at the sack. She slowly pried the top of the bag open. As she looked inside, her eyes grew large. She couldn't believe what she saw! The sack no longer contained the bone of Weenuk's finger, instead it contained the claw of the Great Bear.

With a satisfied and thankful look upon her face, she looked up at the sky first, then at Tom. "Things will be okay. Weenuk has made it so!"

She quickly closed the sack, and hung it once again around her neck.

Tom began noticing slight movements on both sides of the trail, and Nellie knew right away who made the movements. If she had come alone, there would have been great rejoicing, but now that she brought a white man with her, the spirits were uneasy. In fact, they could become deadly at the slightest provocation.

Her old village was just around the bend, and Nellie knew that the spirits would not allow Tom to pass until they felt safe.

"Whoa!" Nellie said as she pulled back on the reins. "Here Tom, wear this. The spirits are uneasy." She took the sack from around her neck and slid it over his.

"What's in this, anyhow?" Tom always wondered, but never bothered to ask.

"Weenuk's finger is now a bear claw," she said without thinking.

"What?" Tom jumped excitedly as he pulled the sack away from his chest.

"It will protect you! No harm shall come to you!"

"You mean, I could have been harmed before?" Tom was really scared now. "My God, what did I get myself into?"

"Shhhhh . . . ." Nellie whispered softly, and Tom instantly obeyed.

The sound of Jimmy's cough broke the tensions, and they both remembered why they were there. Each of their coughs had diminished, but Jimmy's was now much deeper than either of theirs, and he coughed more often.

"Let's do what we came to do and then get out of here." Tom's nervous voice rang out.

The empty field waved its long grasses and the soft wind blew in their direction. The horses' nostrils flared and their ears pointed forward, listening for the slightest noise. The air was heavy, and the breeze carried with it the chill of the spirits. The horses knew the source of the cold winds, just as they knew the taste of the grasses from their homeland. They understood the sacredness of this land, and they were hesitant to enter.

Tom and Nellie jumped off the wagon, pulled out the bed for the pyre, and laid it upon the sacred ground. Next, Tom pulled out the posts and shovels.

"Show me where you want me to dig the holes. Quick! I want to dig these holes and get out of here as soon as we can."

Suddenly, a flood of visions swept over Nellie, and she reeled from the impact. She saw the village exactly as it was the day she left. There were several people walking around, and she could smell soup cooking over the fires. There were children playing and women talking, and a pair of hunters were carrying a deer on their shoulders. No one seemed to notice or care that she was there.

Then all at once, they stopped what they were doing and looked straight at her. They faced her with their hands at their sides. Their eyes were empty and their complexions were sallow. They stood silently and their faces were expressionless. Their spirits were beyond Tom's vision, but he felt their presence.

Jimmy's cough seemed to startle them. The women began walking towards them, and then everyone else followed behind.

"They look scary, Ma!" Jimmy said with a shaky voice.

Nellie hadn't thought about Jimmy being able to see them, but she really wasn't that surprised.

"What's he looking at?" Tom's voice sounded more afraid than Jimmy's.

"He's looking at the people of my village. They are afraid of us."

"They are afraid of us? Hell, they ought to see how afraid I am of them!" Tom spoke loudly.

The spirits now completely surrounded the family. Tom wasn't able to see how close they were, which Nellie knew was a blessing.

"He'd be half way home by now, if he could see them," she thought to herself.

Nellie picked up two of the poles and started walking towards the center of the field. Tom was very close behind, and Jimmy walked between them.

"Here. This is where we need to build it." Nellie said, as she dropped the poles to the ground.

Tom dropped his poles, too, and stood for a second looking at the wagon. He forgot the shovels in the back of the wagon. He hesitated and looked at Nellie

"It's okay. They won't harm you. They see Weenuk's pouch around your neck and know that you are a friend."

Tom sighed in relief, but he still hesitated a second before he walked back to the wagon.

The spirits sat and stood in the tall grass, as they watched the family wandering through the grass that now concealed their bones. The pyre stood nearly six feet tall. The branches were tightly woven inside the end posts. Since it took a long time to assemble a pyre, the spirits waited patiently as Nellie put on the finishing touches. Her people had used the same design, and they were comfortable with the old ways. They knew that the pyre had been built to appease them.

Tom thought it would be easy to find the villagers' bones

scattered on the ground. Unfortunately, due to the tall grass, their task wasn't an easy one. They had to carefully hunt for each and every bone. Their task was made more difficult by the fact that the wolves and other scavengers had eaten some of the bones. However, to their surprise, they recovered most of the bones.

The search lasted until nearly sundown. Once the bones were discovered, they were carefully gathered and placed on the pyre. Before long, the pile of bones and skulls was quite high. It truly was a morbid sight.

Nellie counted twenty-seven different groups of bones, and many of them belonged to children. She held each skull in her hands and thought about to whom it belonged. As she made her discoveries, the spirits came forward and nodded to her in appreciation. Their eyes now expressed peace.

Nellie prepared a temporary shelter for them and rolled out their bedrolls. Although she had plenty of space to work with, she still placed the bedrolls close together. The shelter was downwind from the pyre. Since the fire had to burn an entire day, the smoke would be intense. The aroma from the burning bones would be strong and unpleasant.

In contrast to Tom's nervousness, Jimmy was not at all anxious about being among so many spirits. In fact, he liked being with them. He never had so many playmates, and it didn't matter if he couldn't touch them.

The following day, they had to cut the wood and prepare the fire. So with some time to spare that evening, Nellie, Tom and Jimmy headed over to the river for a swim.

"That water has got to be colder than ice. Hell, the ice hasn't even been gone for more than a few weeks. Are you sure you want to swim in it? Can't we just wash up?" Tom asked, after he put his foot in the water.

Nellie laughed at him as she stood naked on the river's bank. "Catch me if you can boys!" she shouted as she dove in.

That was all Jimmy needed to hear. He quickly dove into the

water and followed his mother. Tom, on the other hand, stood waiting to see their reactions before he jumped in. Truth is he wasn't much of a swimmer, and he liked being able to stand up in the water. This river, however, was very deep.

He cautiously entered the cold river. The cold nipped at his feet, then his knees and thighs. "Oh, damn!" he mumbled to himself, as the icy cold water reached his groin. He continued to inch his way into the water, slowly and surely.

Nellie's legs were powerful and they propelled her quickly to the depths of the river, but when she reached the bottom, she quickly ran out of air. She twisted her body and pushed hard against the bottom, and like a spear, she shot to the water's surface.

Just as she broke through and gasped for air, Tom plunged in. With a whoop that would scare any spirit, he bobbed up and down like a cork. The icy cold water grasped him firmly and numbed his senses. Within a few minutes, he was enjoying himself, moving his arms in circles to keep himself afloat.

Nellie laughed at him, and with cupped hands, splashed him soundly.

"You cut that out, now, you hear? I'm not much of a swimmer!"

With a laugh, she splashed him again, then turned and dove underwater.

The cold water clung to Jimmy's skin and startled his senses, as he swam close to the water's edge. He hung onto the small bushes planted along the river's bank, while he watched his parents swimming. His mother swam like the fishes and his father paddled like a dog.

Tom continued to whoop and holler, even after his body became accustomed to the river's coldness. The water's power filled his body and charged his spirit. Now he understood Nellie's compulsion to return to the river. He had never felt more alive or closer to his family.

# Chapter 19

Nellie's feet pounded on the Earth, as she shook her rattle towards the dark sky. Tom maintained a steady beat on the drum, while Jimmy chanted along. Their sounds were crisp and clear, and echoed through the night. Nellie danced hard, and her voice was carried by the Snowy Owl to Manitou, himself. Her message was one of great importance and she wanted it delivered at once.

Her sounds wailed as her dancing intensified. Tom kept the drum beat moving to her footsteps. She swirled again and again, as she danced around the pyre. She held a torch up high, and its light cast off bazaar shadows on the ground.

Their voices were soon joined by the voices of the dead spirits, because they were anxious to get home. The spirits encircled the pyre, and everyone's voices blended together in perfect harmony. The wailing gradually increased in volume, pitch and tempo.

The ancestors gathered together and watched from above. They were all awakened by the calls from below. They soon joined in with the others.

With a tremendous boom, the Great Bear appeared and stood proudly in front of everyone. He towered above the others, nearly the height of three men. His body was thick and his legs were massive. He stood on his hind legs and swept his razor sharp claws through the air. He roared once again and his thunder shook the Earth.

Invigorated by Manitou's voice, their voices continued to rise. The sounds of thunder awakened Mother Earth, and with a spectacular display of her power, she flashed lightning on the

Earth. The brilliance filled the skies. Even the Spirit of the River joined in and the river's current increased.

Nellie's feet pounded on the Earth, as she swirled and danced. She held her hands high in the air and her hair blew wildly in the wind. Bending down, she passed the torch close to the kindling and caught the sticks on fire. Soon the flames spread rapidly, engulfing the neatly stacked tower of timber.

The Great Bear roared and Mother Earth flashed her powerful lightning. The winds brought the rain, which came down in torrents. The brilliance of the flames completely filled the blackness of night.

The spirits sang with all of their hearts, as the flames reached higher. At first, only a single bone began to smolder, but eventually all of the bones began to burn. The released energy turned into a column of light that reached high into the heavens. The light intensified, as the pyre crumbled into the flames and the bones ignited in a brilliant flash.

Father Moon looked down and watched with great interest, and like a great mirror, he reflected the brilliant beam of light to the crown of ice that covered the far North. From the purity of the light, the midnight sky became luminescent with this brilliance. From distances far and wide, the Northern Lights lit the skies with an amazing display.

The spirits became drawn into the light, and with a final flash, they simply vanished.

The morning sun woke the birds of the bush and they sang sweetly. The Eagle, Hawk and Snowy Owl felt relieved, because now they only had three people to watch over.

Tom was quite anxious to leave the field and return home. He had had enough excitement to last him a lifetime. He watched the evening's spectacle in awe, but was glad when it was finally over. Now he and his family could return home. They finished their morning meal quickly and packed up the wagon.

Nellie thought about her friends and their final journey to the land of their ancestors. She felt good that she was able to send them home, but now she felt alone. The place she had always considered her true home, no longer had any meaning to her. She was now riding away from it, forever. She remained quiet as the wagon rattled its way back home. In fact, everyone was silent. The only sound that broke the silence was an occasional cough.

"Do you think they're happy now?" Tom asked without looking at Nellie.

He stared blankly. He thought about what he had witnessed and how it impacted his life. With a single flash of light, everything he believed in vanished, and a whole new world of truths filled his mind.

"Do you think everyone has a God?" He began probing for answers to his many questions.

"Did you ever see such lightning?" His voice got excited. "I haven't ever seen anything like that before. Not ever."

Tom, Nellie and Jimmy continued to visit the river regularly. As their visits increased in frequency, Jimmy's skills as a swimmer also increased. The power of the river worked well in reducing their coughs, but as soon as they left the water, their coughs persisted.

Since most of the settlers and loggers believed that the village was haunted, they never came around. As a result, Nellie and Tom had their own quiet spot to enjoy. Although they liked their seclusion, they also realized that they needed to build a lodge to protect themselves from the weather. Despite their interest in building a lodge, they had neither the hides nor the strength to do it, so they settled on a temporary shelter. At first, Tom resented having to leave his cabin, because it held so many happy memories. But eventually, he found his new way of life enjoyable, and his happiness increased.

The Spirit of the River worked long and hard to relieve their coughs, but its effectiveness began to wane. Jimmy's cough had become much worse, and he rarely slept soundly. Chief du Fond and Weenuk began visiting him frequently while he slept. Council meetings were held more often, and the ancestors watched with grave concern.

The treatments and remedies were no longer effective, and all three of them began to lose their energy. Since Jimmy's night cough became constant, Nellie rarely slept. As a result, her eyes became sunken and dull.

Tom maintained their supply of game and fish, but even in her weakened state, she did not allow him to cook. Now that she was in her homeland, she wanted to honor the ways of her people.

As their strength diminished, the council meetings were held more often. In fact, they were held almost every night.

Weenuk prepared a surprise for both Jimmy and Tom, but he didn't want anyone else but the Chief to know about it. With the Chief's help, he spoke to Manitou and received His approval to hold a naming ceremony.

It was no longer necessary for Nellie, Tom and Jimmy to chant to the ancestors, since they were always present with them. However, since they liked to follow tradition, they continued to drum and chant aloud.

Covered with his bearskin robe, Weenuk stood in his youthful pride. He had finally made a decision about his age, and he chose thirty years old. His hair was tied on the left side, and he displayed two Eagle feathers. His arms were powerful and his eyes gleamed with wisdom.

Before too long, the ancestors grabbed Jimmy and Tom by the hands and had them dance for everyone. At first, Tom felt silly and out of place, but eventually he began to enjoy himself as much as the others.

The fire rose up and cast an eerie light. The drummer's beat continued to increase with the pounding of their feet. They sang to the spirits and soon everyone was present.

Weenuk held his hands up to the heavens, while both Jimmy and Tom stood before him. First, he rested his hand on Tom's shoulder and said, "My friends and ancestors, you all know why we have gathered. I speak out in the words of Manitou. He has the spirit of our blood and the heart of the wolf. From this day forth he shall be called Watahaha, Two Claws."

The ancestors' voices rang out in happiness, then Weenuk took Jimmy by the hand and turned him around to face the others. "Now our hearts smile, and I bring forth our warrior. Manitou, Great Spirit and Keeper of All Knowledge, I call upon you this day. Before me is this child that has lived in the world of the white man. He has spoken often in council, and his heart is pure and his mind is strong. The child has earned the right to receive the name of a man, despite his young age. From his day forth he shall be called Naheshna-hea, Spirit Swimmer. All shall know this name and respect it, for it is an honorable name."

Everyone joined in the festivities, and their voices echoed throughout the bush. Before too long, Tom, Nellie and Jimmy became tired and fell asleep on the ground.

Tom's dreams were filled with memories of a life that he had never known. He spoke to others in a language that was similar to Nellie's. Was his spirit really an Indian? His dream began with him sitting around a fire pit with others. Then he was hunting with a bow and spoke softly to a friend. He saw a village that had several lodges, where people walked freely around. He slept next to a woman who was stout, but still looked very much like Nellie. Then he was a warrior charging after a band of enemies.

When he woke from his dreams, it was still night. It took his eyes a while to get accustomed to the darkness. He put both hands behind his head and looked at the black sky. His world had changed so drastically in the past few months. The home and livelihood that had taken him a lifetime to achieve, were no more. They just didn't matter to him. He had a new life with Nellie and Jimmy. But now, the two most precious people in his life were deteriorating before his very eyes, and all he could do was to stand by and watch.

He didn't really understand how much his family meant to Weenuk and the others until he came to the old Montagnais village. He now understood her connection to Manitou and the other spirits. He didn't know why Weenuk chose him, but he did know that Weenuk's love for Nellie was at least equal to his own. However, there was no way that he could ever give up Nellie to Weenuk or any other man. Now that he had found her, he could never let her go.

His thoughts went back to Jimmy. He knew that Weenuk's spirit was connected to his son, but he not only accepted this fact, he was very thankful for it. If it hadn't had been for Weenuk, Jimmy probably would have been dead already.

He turned to Nellie and put his arm around her, hugging her softly. Surprisingly, she responded by turning to face him. He tried to speak, but she pressed her fingers to his lips and whispered, "Now you understand our love, and the love for our child. You already know the answers to your questions, but sleep now, and they will all come to you."

She kissed his lips tenderly and wrapped her arms around him. She snuggled her head against his chest and entwined her legs with his. They tenderly made love and then drifted back to sleep.

Jimmy loved his new name, and after several attempts he finally pronounced it correctly. Naheshna-hea suited him just fine. For the next several days, Tom kept forgetting to use their Indian names, and his son often scolded him. Now Ma and Pa were replaced with Wishna-hea and Watahaha.

The summer was almost over and Naheshna-hea's cough worsened steadily. He no longer had the strength to swim, but he enjoyed feeling the refreshing coolness of the water on his skin. The Spirit of the River did its best to heal him, but the young boy's days were numbered.

As Naheshna-hea weakened, his parents became concerned. They sat around the fire pit and called the ancestors. The flames leaped into the blackness of night and a blanket of clouds hid the stars.

The ancestors watched with intensity, as Weenuk danced for Naheshna-hea. His heart beat strongly and he danced feverishly around the boy's bed. His voice became fierce, and he shouted out boldly to the Evil One, "You have beaten me for the last time! Now you are going to feel the teeth of Weenuk."

Chief du Fond sat anxiously. He was prepared to grant his spirit to Weenuk, if he needed it. Although Naheshna-hea and the Chief existed on different plains of life, the Chief could offer his spirit so that the young boy could live.

Weenuk's spiritual body bore the scars of many battles. His mind was sharp and his reflexes were ready. He was prepared for the final battle.

Weenuk bellowed, "Come, and sit beside me, and we shall smoke the pipe of friendship, my mighty and greatest foe!"

# Chapter 20

"You speak with the tongue of a serpent! How dare you offer me the pipe of friendship and then call me your enemy. I cannot be both. Which do you offer me now?" The Evil One spat.

"I am new to this land of spirits, and I offer all who sit before me the pipe of friendship. Isn't it better to discuss our differences than to wage an all out war?" Weenuk chose his words carefully.

"You fear me, you coward, for I have beaten you like a dog!"

A bolt of lightning struck the Evil One squarely in the chest and drove him onto his back. Weenuk's eyes were filled with fire and he grew to an immense size. Before the Evil One could catch his breath, two more bolts scorched his spirit, and he reeled in pain. A force stronger than the wind blasted Weenuk and thrust him far behind.

"You have yet to feel my teeth, and I shall make you cringe in pain!" Weenuk shouted defiantly.

With a groan, The Evil One whipped a ball of fire at Weenuk's head. This was his favorite weapon, and he used it skillfully.

A tremendous burst of rain erupted from the clouds and doused the fiery ball.

"I have learned your way of battle, and have defenses against your worse weapons. Now speak with me in friendship or I shall destroy you quickly. I am not a vengeful spirit, and I prefer friendship to hate. I shall not ask again." Weenuk spoke strongly and his eyes were as cold as ice.

With a violent dive, The Evil One struck out at Weenuk's throat.

Weenuk easily blocked his attempt and swung at him with all of his might. He caught the Evil One on the jaw, and sent him reeling backwards.

Just as Weenuk was about to scream another challenge, two giant snakes coiled around his legs and held him fast. The Evil One hurled his snake spear directly at Weenuk's heart.

Weenuk's medicine shield protected him from the incoming spear. He then used it to sever the two snakes wrapped around his legs. Before the pieces could hit the ground, they turned into mountain lions, and quickly sprang towards Weenuk's eyes.

He used the medicine shield to block the first one, but the second one came from behind, so he had no defense against it. As the lion hurled Weenuk's body forward, it dug its claws deep into Weenuk's flesh. He swung his shield and severed lion's leg, then he snatched the lion's throat in his hands, and ripped its windpipe out.

Just then, another lion pounced on his back, followed by another, then another, then another. With a flash of light, the cats were blinded. They tore savagely at anything they could get their claws on. Before they knew it, they had shredded each other into a gnarled mass of flesh and blood.

Weenuk stumbled to his knees, but he wouldn't back down from the Evil One.

"Your petty weapons bore me. I thought they said you were good!" His words cut like a spear.

Naheshna-hea's fever was raging, and deep coughs ripped from his lungs. Sweat poured from his body. Wishna-hea held him closely and frantically rocked him back and forth, while Watahaha dumped bucket after bucket of the healing waters over them, trying to break his fever. Wishna-hea was far too weak to hold him in the water, and her strength was needed to keep him in the human world.

His small body convulsed with each cough, and everyone was frantic.

The battle raged on in darkness. Sparks flashed, blows crashed and blood soon covered the land. Manitou called forth the dawn, revealing a badly bloodied pair. Weenuk and the Evil One didn't seem to notice Manitou's presence, so they continued their frenzied battle. Weenuk proved his cunning and power, as the Evil One thrashed out with all of his might and vengeance. With each new assault, Weenuk's resolve was tested again and again.

The Evil One was furious that another spirit could withstand his fury, and still be able to draw his blood. He attacked viciously, but Weenuk blocked and countered every attempt.

Fed up, the Evil One unleashed his final attack. The Earth's surface opened and a spray of molten lava knocked Weenuk to his knees. In an instant, the Evil One hurled a tremendous stone, catching Weenuk squarely in the face, driving him to the ground.

And with a final gasp for air, Naheshna-hea's lungs collapsed and ceased to breathe.

"You have proven your cunning and power, but it is I who reign supreme." The voice of the Evil One spat. "I have taken your son from you, and with it, I take the future of your people." His evil laugh could be heard far and wide.

Wishna-hea clutched her son's lifeless body, and wailed from deep within. Tears poured from her eyes, as Watahaha crumbled to his knees, reaching for them as he fell to the ground. A great sadness covered the land, and the black cloud of death once again covered their home.

The ancestors sat speechless, as they watched in total dismay. Their hope for the future was gone. He was snatched from them before he had a chance to live.

Watahaha and Wishna-hea prepared the pyre according to

tradition, and the ancestors sat patiently waiting for their friend to arrive. Watahaha beat rhythmically on the drum, as Wishna-hea danced around the small pyre, chanting loudly.

*"With my deepest sadness I swooped down from above and carried the words back to Manitou's home to tell the Ancestors. Weenuk had regained enough strength to sit with his friend. They both sat in silence. It was time for the young spirit to return to their home. I lowered my head as I stood there waiting. There was no need for words, just mournful regrets. My duties would soon be over. There was but a single flight left to make."*

The midnight sky was black and the winds howled. Thunder roared and lightning flashed. The rains came down like rivers. The Earth trembled with the sounds of thunder, as Manitou displayed his might. Again and again the lightning struck the trees, bursting them into flames. Harder and harder the rain came down, and the winds increased their strength.

Wishna-hea took the doll of her childhood, and placed it upon her son's lap. She leaned forward and pressed her lips against his. Watahaha couldn't control his sobs. It was not the Indian way to display such emotions, but his woman was sure the spirits would overlook it. He buried his head into his son's small chest, and the tears flooded out.

After a short time, Wishna-hea pulled him gently back and said, "No man could ever have been a better father, but it is now time for him to take his final journey." Reluctantly, Watahaha stood up and his tears dried on his cheek.

"Why couldn't the spirits have taken me?" He looked at Wishna-hea with grief and puzzlement.

"It was his time to go to the ancestors. He had served his purpose on Earth well." Watahaha knew that she was close to breaking down, but somehow she maintained her composure.

With no other words, she touched the torch to the kindling, and the flames leaped upward, enveloping the pyre, which had been built in the center of the small cabin. Within moments the air had been sucked out of the bereaved parents lungs, and once again all three spirits had been joined together. The flames were whipped into a frenzy by the winds, as they climbed onto the back of the magnificent Eagle. After a moment of settlement Wishna-hea kicked the ribs of the magnificent bird and in close embrace the three began their journey home. Higher and higher the flames reached, almost touching the sky.

It wasn't long before Naheshna-hea looked at his father. "Look! Look at Daddy!"

He turned to his mother, and his eyes got even bigger. "Daddy! Look at Mommy!" Miraculously, before his very eyes, both his parents arms began growing feathers, and began stretching out. All three watched the other two in amazement, as arms became wings, and bodies began their transformation. Voices became screeches, and noses became beaks, as the skies became blessed with three more magnificent eagles.

The wind caught the flames and spread the fire to the hayfield, then to the trees. Soon the bush land of the Montagnais was blackened by fire.

Earth became replenished as their flesh turned to ash, and their spirits were set free. Their wings carried them swiftly together on their final flight home.

The wisdom of Manitou, once again proved infinite. Just as the Mighty Bear sleeps in the season of the snows, the hope of the Montagnais went into a deep sleep.

# ABOUT THE AUTHOR

The writing of *Through The Eye of the Eagle* began more than seven years ago. At that time I was living in a small town in Connecticut, and through a spiritual connection I was led more than a thousand miles away, to Northern Ontario, and eventually to Eau Claire Gorge. There I was introduced to the spirit of Wishna-hea herself. By no means was there any subtly to this introduction. She came to me with a power that was so consuming that I found myself clinging to an ancient White Pine, that leaned precariously out over the Gorge itself. From the depths of me came a scream that was muffled only by the roar of the gorge, itself, as this strange energy overwhelmed me.

A short time later, I left my home in Connecticut to live on the lands where Wishna-hea once called her home. After my first long Canadian winter, in near isolation on the pristine Smith Lake, the book was nearly completed. Day by day, I shared in the agonies and ecstasies of Wishna-hea as I hammered away at depicting the legend, as only she would have told it. Upon nearing the completion of the book, I became filled with dread as the predictable ending that I had envisioned vanished. Instead, the story concluded exactly as the lives of the characters really had, tragically, but yet filled with hope.

The writing of *Through The Eye of the Eagle, the Legend of Eau Claire Gorge,* was the beginning of my spiritual enlightment. It started with gaining an understanding of Native Spirituality but soon led me to the path of my Celtic ancestry where I discovered many of secrets of the *Sacred Teachings*. These teaching were opened to me for the purpose of sharing with others their complexity, but also their simplicity. I extend an invitation to you that will enable you to explore the possibilities that become opened through a greater spiritual understanding.

At *Eye of the Eagle Retreat* we conduct teaching circles and workshops that are hosted by many others, as well as myself. To learn more about these workshops and also the progress of my new upcoming books check out our website: www.eyeoftheeagle.net

Thanks for allowing me the opportunity to let you view history from a different perspective.

ISBN 1-41205783-3